"*Speak to any gay man about his childhood and he will tell you a story of joy and discovery — like any other child. But read between the lines and you will find a testament of pain and the struggle to find a place in the world. This needn't be the case...*

The message of Love Me As I Am will hopefully be heard by every parent, teacher, lover and employer to help them realise how homophobia, even in its slightest suggestion, can impact the lives of those at the receiving end of it."

Joe Kort, Ph.D., Psychotherapist and author of *10 Smart Things Gay Men Can Do to Improve Their Lives*

LOVE ME
AS I AM

gay men reflect on their lives

LOVE ME AS I AM Copyright © 2012 Published by The Quest

For contact information visit: www.thequestawaitsyou.com

UK Retail Price: £9.99
Recommended categories:
Gay & Lesbian | Gender Studies | Self Help | Gay Biography/Autobiography

Printed in the United Kingdom
Printed by CPI Books UK
First Print, October 2012
Design and layout by Francois Lubbe
Cover design by Francois Lubbe

ISBN-10: 0957330103
ISBN-13: 978-0957330108

A catalogue record of this book is available from the British Library

Contact information for the Publisher, The Quest, can be found at:
www.thequestawaitsyou.com

All profits gained by the Publisher, The Quest, through the sales of 'Love Me As I Am', will be donated to Diversity Role Models:
Charity number: 1142548

For more information on Diversity Role Models visit:
www.diversityrolemodels.org

'Love Me As I Am' is an anthology of the writings by 24 contributing authors, who have given their full consent for publication. Opinions expressed herein are not necessarily that of the Publisher. The anthology has been curated and overseen by the Co-Founders of The Quest, Ade Adeniji and Darren Brady, and Editor Francois Lubbe.

LOVE ME AS I AM
gay men reflect on their lives

Dedicated to gay men everywhere in the world who at some point in their lives have felt the pain of not belonging. May you find a voice for your untold stories and a place to call home.

CONTENTS

"Often, it's not about becoming a new person, but becoming the person you were meant to be, and already are, but don't know how to be."
Heath L. Buckmaster

INTRODUCTION

In autumn 2010, the UK gay lifestyle magazine *Attitude* featured a cover story on gay men's mental health. This issue, titled the 'Issues Issue', explored self-esteem problems, depression, addictions and substance abuse amongst gay men. It took its premise from the bestselling book *The Velvet Rage* by Alan Downs and looked at the experiences and journeys of a cross-section of gay men. It was a groundbreaking edition, especially since *Attitude* is better known for featuring half-naked men with perfect bodies, instead of discussing the real challenges faced by the gay community.

The 'Issues Issue' put the debate on gay men's emotional and mental wellbeing in the spotlight of mainstream gay culture as the front cover proudly declared, 'We've found the secret to being gay and happy.'

In the following year, *Attitude* followed up their 'Issues Issue' with a panel discussion at the Drill Hall in London. The event featured a few gay men recovering from various forms of addiction. They were joined by a couple of mental health professionals who led the discussion, as they openly talked about the challenges they faced throughout their lives.

We were both deeply moved by the raw honesty of the speakers and saddened by the statistics that told us what we already knew: despite the fact that gay men have come such a long way in facing the challenges of social prejudice and being more visible in mainstream culture, we now had to face ourselves and deal with the emotional residue that had been numbed out and hidden. After the discussion there was a sense of urgency in our conversation as we started to explore what we could do to help the gay community move forward.

As gay men and trained coaches, we both felt a responsibility to help create a safe environment where gay men could come together and explore who they truly are, whilst cultivating intimacy with themselves and other gay men in the process. Our minds and hearts were set on working together to develop a workshop for gay men based on the fundamentals of Alan Downs' book, *The Velvet Rage*. We got in touch with Alan Downs, who gave us the okay to use the title of his book for our workshop.

'Journeying with The Velvet Rage', our inaugural workshop, ran in the summer of 2011 for six consecutive weeks. It was held in the upper lounge of a gay bar in Vauxhall, one of London's famous gay districts. The charity 'Living Well', which works with people living with HIV/AIDS, expressed an interest in the workshop and sponsored more than half of the participants who joined us.

It was a moving and powerful experience as we journeyed along with our first ten participants, as they explored how their upbringings had impacted on their emotional development, and how this affected their lives as adults. The men opened up, discussed and shared their experiences — both devastating and triumphant — in ways we had never witnessed before. This was a testament to us, that gay men were willing to step forward and start exploring living an enhanced and fulfilled life. We had our work cut out.

Shortly after our first workshop, we redesigned the sessions and started to run them over weekends under the title 'The Velvet Rage Weekend Exploration'. Since then, many doors have opened for us. We found a permanent venue, generously provided by GMFA — the London-based gay men's health charity, and the participants of our workshops are confidently starting to build a community of their own. We're also getting emails from people around the country and the world who are curious about what we are doing.

As a result, The Quest was born. The name encapsulates the journey we all embark on as human beings, regardless of our sexual orientation: The Quest to rediscover our true Self, to 'follow our bliss' and to live our own authentic life.

In January 2012, we ran our first weekend exploration workshop under the banner of 'The Quest for Gay Men' and continue to do so. The men who are sharing their stories in Love Me As I Am attended either our inaugural session or one of the follow-up weekend exploration workshops.

Storytelling forms a significant part of our work. In fact, that's how Love Me As I Am came to life. During our workshops, we usually invite the guys to write a letter to their 16-year-old selves. Afterwards, we ask them to share their letters with one other person in the group. It was during one of these sharing exercises that all the guys decided to read their letters in front of the entire group.

The participants found this process to be therapeutic and healing. It allowed them to reconnect with their younger selves, from whom many of them had disconnected a long time ago. During a conversation with the participants, one of them suggested that the letters should be collated into a book for gay teenagers. We all loved the idea of creating a book, and felt that the letters illustrated how there is life and hope after a painful adolescence.

Since those early discussions, the book developed into more than just letters and now includes a short biography of each contributor. The biographies set the scene for the letters and provide a reflection on what the lives of these men were like before and after adolescence.

Although there are common themes in all of the stories in *Love Me As I Am*, it was necessary to divide the contributions into chapters to help the reader understand the journey so many gay men go through. We have written a short introduction to each chapter. We alternated the writing of the chapters. Whilst you might get a flavour of our individual voices, the essence of the introductions is a joint one.

We start off with *Oddly Out Of Place* in which the contributors share what it was like being 'different' or 'the outsider' and their yearning for belonging.

Developing Limiting Beliefs focusses on the beliefs they developed about themselves as a result of feeling oddly out of place, and *Striving To Survive* explains how they put coping strategies in place to help navigate their experience and reaction to the world while masking their limiting beliefs.

Finding The Way Home is about when the realisation kicks in that the coping mechanisms they have developed as gay men no longer satisfy and there is a yearning to thrive rather than simply survive.

These stages are all parts of the chapters in the journey of a gay man's life. The stories in *Love Me As I Am* could easily fit anywhere into this book as they carry the echoes of each stage to a lesser or greater degree.

Finally, in *Moving Forward Authentically*, we explore what happens after we gain clarity about our limiting beliefs and survival strategies: how do we sustain that momentum as we move forward?

Since one of the intentions of the book is to be a catalyst for healing, we understand that the life experiences shared in *Love Me As I Am* may prompt gay men to look for support in the challenges they are facing so we've added a resource section to help gay men find support.

From the onset, we wanted *Love Me As I Am* to be more than just another book in the Gay Section of a bookshop. It certainly has the potential to impact positively on the lives of many people. However, we also want the book to contribute to the broader gay community. This is why everyone involved in creating *Love Me As I Am* agreed that all profits gained by The Quest through the sales of the book should go to a charity that works with young people around the topic of diversity and sexuality.

In our search to find the right charity, we came across the moving story of Dominic Crouch who committed suicide following homophobic bullying at school. Dominic's story was even more heart-breaking because after Dominic's suicide, his father Roger became an avid campaigner against homophobic bullying. Sadly, Roger also committed suicide.

If ever we needed a reminder of the commitment we had for this project, Dominic's story was it.

Before his death, Roger was involved with Diversity Role Models, a UK charity that actively seeks to prevent homophobic bullying in schools in the UK. We met up with Suran Dickson, the CEO of Diversity Role Models, and subsequently chose it as the designated charity to benefit from the sales of *Love Me As I Am*.

We hope that as you join the contributors on their journey, you will reconnect with your own adolescence and recognise the voice inside all of us that simply says: Love me as I am.

Ade Adeniji & Darren Brady
Founders, The Quest for Gay Men
September 2012

MESSAGE FROM DIVERSITY ROLE MODELS

Many years ago, a teacher friend of mine approached me and asked for some advice on how to tackle homophobia in her class as some of her male students were vehemently homophobic. She explained that students had no gay person to relate to and didn't care who they might offend with their behaviour because they saw homosexuality simply as a distant concept that was not connected to any 'real people'.

Having been openly gay with many of my students during my teaching career with no negative backlash, I offered to speak to her students. After showing a jeering, mocking class of 15-year-old boys and girls a slideshow of well-known Lesbian, Gay, Bisexual, and Transgender (LGBT) people, I told them that I was 'one of them', a lesbian.

The room went quiet, there was some indiscreet nudging and eventually the boy closest to me got out of his seat in disgust and moved to the back of the classroom. In that moment, things changed. Another student, who incidentally had been extremely vocal in his belief that homosexuality was an immoral choice, moved to take his place and said, "I'll sit by you, Miss. He's just being a dickhead." The students then started to ask questions. I did my best to answer them, and a lot of the time we had a laugh. They related to me, they understood when I said I didn't choose to be gay, and that I'd been just as confused about my own sexuality when I was 15, as they were.

During the class, not one of the girls said anything. At one point, a male student said, "We don't mind about YOU, but if you were a man we would smash you.": a sure-fire indicator of how much work there was still to be done. It was a life-changing day for me, for the students and for their teacher.

I realised that these conversations were essential for every young person, in every school, in every town, across the UK. All young people are curious about sexuality and for many of them, including those who are lesbian, gay and bisexual, most of the messages they hear are negative and contribute to an environment in which gay students feel out of place, and their straight peers feel their bullying behaviour or mocking words are justified.

The suicide of Dominic Crouch was the final impetus for me to leave my teaching job and set up the charity Diversity Role Models. For Dominic, being called gay gave him enough reason to end his life. In every workshop, we talk about Dominic, and we help students understand the potential implications of homophobic bullying.

Aside from telling Dominic's tragic story, we keep it positive. We usually take two role models into the class, along with a trained facilitator. The role models tell the class a personal story, perhaps about their coming out, their transition, their career paths and their families. We have discussions with students about how they would feel if one of their friends came out to them, to whom they would turn for support if they were being bullied and why they think homophobic bullying exists.

We also give the students the opportunity to ask questions. Most of them want to know how we knew we were gay, why we are like this, how our families reacted, whether we want children and the old can of worms: how will we 'make' children?

Occasionally we get thoughtful queries like: "How do you feel when people stare at you in the street just because you are different?" These children are curious. Once we give them a safe space to ask questions and they relate to us as human beings, they are far more empathetic. We challenge them not to target somebody in the street because they suspect they are transgender, gay or just different.

It's always interesting to observe that at the beginning of our workshops, 50 per cent of the students say they would stop being friends with a classmate who comes out to them, and at the end only 2 per cent hold onto this viewpoint.

Ninety five per cent of the students we've seen say they would treat an LGBT person better after participating in our workshops. To poignantly demonstrate the impact of our work, a 12-year-old boy once approached our role models after class one day and said: "My dad taught me to cross the street when I see people like you. I now know that is wrong and I'm not going to do it anymore."

I can see no better fit for Diversity Role Models than a project like *Love Me As I Am* which touchingly and at times painstakingly, connects grown men with their boy-selves, asking them to go easy on themselves and letting them know that life will get better. This book corresponds exquisitely with our work. Diversity Role Models connects with young people; helps them to understand that people are different, asks them to be gentle with each other and to remember, above all, that love is love and need not provoke anger or bullying in anyone.

Suran Dickson
Chief Executive
Diversity Role Models
www.diversityrolemodels.org

CHAPTER ONE

ODDLY OUT OF PLACE

Listening to the stories people tell about their very early childhoods, it's difficult to ignore the common thread and emphasis on wanting to belong. While this is true for all children, it is particularly pronounced in gay children.

As human beings, we are programmed to make attachments and establish emotional bonds from the day we enter this world; we literally crave 'emotional sustenance'. As babies and children, our survival and wellbeing depends on the emotional nourishment we get from our families. Later in life, as we venture into the world, those early bonds and the sense of security they give us act as guidelines that help us build healthy and supportive relationships of our own.

Most gay children are born into heterosexual families. Consequently, as we grow up, we discover that for some reason, we will probably never marry like our parents did, and we may not be able to build and have a family of our own. This discovery alienates us from the very thing we so desperately want to belong to. Even though we cannot put a name to it yet, we know that we are different long before we can tell anyone else... not even our parents.

In *Oddly Out Of Place*, the stories echo these feelings of being removed from our families and our loved ones. They illustrate how, from a very early age, we notice our own detachment from the rich and exciting landscape that unfolds before our eyes.

It's a landscape in which there is no reference to what we are looking for; it's not in the stories we are told, the parents we meet, the conversations we hear or the voices that speak to us. It is a subtle but significant, silent and often unconscious lack of acknowledgement.

For the parents of infants and toddlers, their children's sexual development may seem a long way off. However, the truth is that sexual development begins in a child's very early years. Infants, toddlers, preschoolers, and young school-aged children develop an emotional and physical foundation for sexuality in many subtle ways as they grow into their own being.

Even some of the most liberal parents still deem it inappropriate to discuss their child's sexuality until they have reached their teenage years. Those who are more conservative often draw a parallel between talking about a young child's 'sexuality' and 'sex'. They lambast this notion as being sick and depraved. Therefore, the mere thought that a young child might be gay is often too difficult to conceive for some parents, despite the fact that social attitudes are changing in some parts of the world.

The majority of parents still struggle to acknowledge their child's sexuality in the same simple way they would recognise their gender, hair colour and racial or ethnic background. However, for a growing number of people there is no longer a place for the rhetoric of 'nobody is born gay' or 'my child is too young to know about these things'.

In order to create an environment that encourages the healthy expression and exploration of sexuality, we need to accept the fact that children have an inborn sexual preference that will develop over time. Between the ages of 4 and 6, a child's sexuality is not about sex. Instead, it is all about identity. For the gay child, his or her sexual identity is defined by a curiosity and attraction to the same sex in a way that differentiates them from their young heterosexual counterparts.

Just because a boy plays with a toy car doesn't mean he will become a racing driver. In much the same way, when a boy plays with an Action Man, he may not necessarily one day want to enter into a civil partnership with another man. The point is, instead of assuming a child's sexuality, we can listen, watch and respond openly to their uninhibited behaviour — allowing them to play the games they want to play and ask the questions that pop up in their curious minds. By observing them, we will learn rather quickly what their preference might be.

Most gay men remember how they expressed their sexual identity by playing certain games. Others found an outlet through special friendships or being fond of specific characters in stories and on television. All of this happened on a very innocent and non-sexual level, even though subconsciously it was about their sexuality. In a similar vein, parents of gay children will often reflect and say that 'they knew it', that deep down they always felt that their little boy was 'different'. This really is just another way of saying they knew all along he was gay.

Sadly, many parents are still so ashamed, panicked or bewildered by the nature of their child's sexual evolution that they ignore, deny or chastise their child's sexuality. Most parents are too ill-prepared to respond to their child's evolving sexuality. On these shaky foundations and with such conditional love, a gay child is expected to develop a sense of self. It is hardly surprising that as gay children we feel alone at best and judged at worse.

While we are nurtured and loved, we are simultaneously also rejected on a very fundamental level. This rejection plants a painful seed inside us that inevitably will grow. As time passes, this seed will perhaps be watered by prejudice, nurtured by ignorance or cultivated by a deafening silence. Our invalidation will be projected onto us with bigoted words and limiting beliefs, and religious and cultural intolerance. This painful seed will certainly flourish in the fertile landscapes of nursery and school playgrounds; children are often much crueller than adults, especially when they perceive someone as being 'different'.

As this seed grows, so does our perception of the unspoken burden inside us. We will respond to this pain in many different ways. Some of us will revel in being different, some will be strong and independent very quickly, and others will withdraw and suppress their young and vibrant spirits. However, the one common thread all gay children share is the painful understanding that we are different and oddly out of place, and for those who love us, this is unacceptable.

*"Don't look back at the past —
you're not going there."*
Anonymous

Phil - 46

I was a happy-go-lucky child. I grew up in a loving, simple household. Suburban London was safe and comfortable — a little dull perhaps, but easy and inextreme. Part of me always wanted to be different — a punk, a troublemaker or hip and trendy, or shocking. I craved attention and fame. However, I'm an introvert, so instead I hung back and melted into the background; I watched the exciting and sexy people from the shadows.

Aged 16, I was still relatively naïve — like a well-behaved puppy: wide eyed, innocent and quiet. I knew I was gay, but it didn't trouble me — and still doesn't. I "practiced" being gay from time to time, and loved sex (I still do). Because I had no choice in choosing my sexuality, I had no sense of embarrassment or shame. For me, my sexuality was my "difference" — my minority and my little bit of rebellion. I liked the fact that I had a "special" quality...

My adult life has been up and down. I have never really been 'on the scene'. I rarely dated and have had three long-term, serious relationships. I'm now single — sometimes happily and sometimes less so. I am often in my own company, and until recently, I have never felt alone. I've worked hard and have been successful in my career, although recently things have taken a downward turn.

The last few years have been difficult. I've had to deal with a horrid relationship breakup, the loss of my parents, financial difficulties, work issues and depression. And then, just when it seemed that things couldn't get any worse — they did. Recently, I have been diagnosed as HIV positive. It was a strange and shocking wake-up call.

Life seems to get tougher as I get older — no-one really warns you about this. I'm at a crossroad in my life. I'm scared and apprehensive about the future, but also slightly excited. Life is for living. At the moment I'm healthy and nearly happy. It could be worse. It could be much, much worse.

Dear Phil,

Phil, you're a quiet and self-contained young man; intelligent and bright. You have a lot to offer. Don't waste the wonderful opportunities that lie ahead. Life can be incredibly exciting. Try and use every moment. Enjoy yourself. Appreciate your life and your family.

Try and work harder at school — push yourself to newer heights. You'll breeze through your 'O' levels — but the next step is a killer. Enjoy your degree, but in your final year, perhaps spend a little less time in the bar, and a little more on your books.

Don't miss out, because you can't be bothered. Make an effort. It's easy to go with the flow, or to give up. Sometimes stop; turn round; go back. Don't regret not doing something. When Andrew, on the Town Planning diploma, rings you out of the blue at work, he is reaching out to you. He wants to talk. Don't brush him off.

Don't look back on the past too much — learn and move on. Enjoy the moment — feel it and take it for what it is. You will naturally look back and wonder why, or wish you hadn't done certain things. It's in your personality to review and keep thinking "what if." But remember, the past has gone, and you're not going there.

Keep in touch with friends. Communicate more. Your college friends are special. Don't let go easily. People love you — let them in and enjoy being loved. You'll appreciate your friends as you get older.

When you know something — when you really feel something, trust yourself. You will be right. You understand more than you know — believe in yourself.

There will be many times when you accommodate other people's wishes in order to keep the peace, or take the easy path... You don't always have to compromise. You are wise. Overcome your head and go with your heart.

Don't hold onto things that you know are finished. Relationships end. People come in and out of our lives for different reasons and for different lengths of time. Celebrate those relationships — don't mourn their passing.

Take risks. Be scared sometimes. You will surprise yourself at how much you enjoy those moments when you step out of your comfort zone. As you get older, it gets harder to change your life path — but if you don't take control, external factors will change it for you. Control your destiny as far as you can.

Finally, tell your parents that you love them. Do it regularly. You will regret NOT telling them one day. You are lucky to have been born into your family. Appreciate that luck sooner, rather than later.

Phil

"When most of us say: 'I can't bear this',
we are proving we can."

Alasdair Gray, 'Lanark'

Gavin - 35

For much of my life I haven't felt at home anywhere. My family moved continents three times and by the time I was 8, we had moved from Scotland to Canada to the Middle East and back to Scotland. I was moved between five different schools in five years — always an incomer, never sure what was required to earn approval and fit in; always the one lacking the local accent and a gang of lifelong friends.

By the time I realised that I might be gay, two things occurred inside me. First, it seemed to make some kind of cosmic sense: here was yet another way I didn't feel at home in a world apparently made to suit others. However, I'm lucky to be able to say that I never ever felt guilt about my sexuality, or felt it was in any way wrong to be gay (I had a very secular upbringing). Secondly, I felt a certain sense of pride.

However, my restless childhood meant I was very unsure of my place in the world and how to express myself publicly, and as a result, I couldn't find the strength, stability or self-confidence to come out for a long time. My lack of courage and character, as

I saw it, led to self-loathing and I began to struggle with anxiety and depression.

I also dreaded how others would react — friends would abandon me, I thought. Anyone who knew of my secret would label me with all the negative gay stereotypes and use it as a filter rather than seeing my own 'me-ness'... whatever that might be. Being shy, I also resented the prospect of having to bare my desires and my bodily urges publicly; straight people didn't have to do it, because heterosexuality is assumed. So, why did I have to declare something so deeply personal to the world? Adolescence is enough of an awkward, self-conscious time even without this mortifying ordeal.

During my teenage years, my father often used derogatory words about gay people — poofter, queer, dyke — and even though I did not properly understand it, I realised he was talking about me. I sensed his hatred was dangerous, and I started to put an emotional distance between him and me, which confused and outraged him.

My mother, a woman of enormous strength and brittle fragility, had a gentler and impeccably liberal outlook, but in some ways her view was just as devastating to my confidence. At around the age of 14, I asked her how she would feel if any of her children were gay. She told me she would be "sad, because it seems like a lonely life". I had already spent my childhood tiptoeing around her sadness, trying not to make it deeper, so this made it even harder to come out to her.

When I left school, I went as far away as possible to university, seeking to leave the school cliques and culture behind — leave myself behind, in fact — and start from scratch. But I spent two years just as paralysed. I would stand outside my housemates' bedroom door with my fist literally raised, poised to knock, trembling. I knew that if I knocked, they would say 'Come in' and I would go in, sit down and tell them I was gay, and the torture would be ended. It only needed my single knock — a simple action, over in a heartbeat. But each time I lost my nerve. I set myself deadlines to come out, and every time they passed and I had not found the courage. My self-hatred deepened.

In my third year, I moved to London for an internship at the House of Commons. Finally, there, I met out gay men. I visited my first gay bars. For the first time, I looked down on a dancefloor full of gay men dancing, kissing, touching, smiling, living — and it remains one of the most beautiful sights I have ever seen.

I had found home for the first time in my life: I don't mean that club, and I don't mean the gay scene, but something inside me that was finally peaceful. I had been holding my breath for 20 years and was now breathing deeply for the first time. I had my first boyfriend that year, lost my virginity and made gay friends. I was soon out to my entire family, who are loving and accepting of me. Even my father is, on the rare occasions that we meet, politely respectful of my sexuality — at least to my face.

Since then, I've had a series of relationships. Most of them were pretty dysfunctional. However, I have been in a monogamous relationship with a man I love for more than seven years now. Still, the toxicity of that early self-hatred has not entirely left me, and it continues to make life a struggle. Our relationship can be painful, because we each bring our own damaged selves to it - but I think it has endured because we both work so hard at recognising this.

However, I am gaining more clarity about the effects of poisonous self-blame. My work now is to forgive myself for what was never really the fault of a boy who was simply badly prepared and poorly nurtured to create his own place in a world built for others.

One of the things that keeps me going is a deep pride and affection for the queer men and women who have grown up in a predominantly heterosexual world. It takes hard work and courage to build your own self-worth in a world that does not tell you 'You are OK as you are'. And though it can be painful, and a lifelong struggle to do so, I really believe that, as gay people, we're privileged to experience the world from our extraordinary point of view.

If I were given the option to go back and choose whether to be born gay or straight, I really would choose to be gay all over again. This time, though, I wouldn't waste a single day hiding.

Dear Gavin,

It will save time and confusion if I tell you now that you are definitely gay. So, there's not much point in having those excruciating, sometimes humiliating experiences with the few girls that you're going to try kissing, to see if it arouses you or feels right.

Come out as soon as possible. The family you care about will be supportive and won't desert you as you fear they will. And it will sort out the real friends from the false, immature or scared ones - and this would be a great gift, which few people are given at your age.

Dad is dad. Angry, a bit homophobic, awkward, a vulnerable and confused bully. He is what he is. If you can make a few older male friends, or even just one, who can mentor and guide you in the way Dad is incapable of, it will do you a world of good.

Your mum is doing her best, but she's not the nurturing type. That's not her fault, or yours. So you're going to have to nurture yourself, care about yourself, and seek out and surround yourself with others who can help with that task — which is a task, believe it or not, that's supposed to be a pleasure! Try to get your head around this.

Get out, meet some boys. Find and join a gay youth group, so you have some peers you can have fun with and learn from, and explore together. Other straight boys your age have their own version of this already - you deserve to have your own. It's a normal and essential part of growing up and figuring out who you are.

The longer you stay in the closet, the less able you will be to express yourself in any and every aspect of your life, and the less confidence you'll have in expressing yourself. That lack of self-expression will become toxic and will cause you at least 20 years of inner pain and suffocation, so take a deep breath and do it. No one else can do it for you. And there is not one thing in your life that will be better by leaving it until later.

Oh. And chill the fuck out. Relax. Have fun. Do things that scare you. The sky will not fall in. Life will have a much richer texture.

With unconditional love,

Gavin

"There is no way to happiness, happiness is the way."
Fernando

Fernando - 42

I am 42 years old and proudly Brazilian. I was born into a very strict Christian Catholic family. Being brought up in a rigidly religious family made my life a living hell and in my little world, I was the most unhappy and lonely kid. Suffering was part of my everyday life and unfortunately, I was too insignificant for anybody to take notice of my hardship. My father was violent towards my mother and my mother retaliated by being callous, abusive and cold-hearted towards her children. My brothers and sisters and I had to bear the brunt of all the frustration and anger she felt towards my father.

I knew I liked boys from a very early age, I just did not know what being gay meant. I thought that gays were 'those guys' who wore dresses and acted like girls — drag queens and transvestites. I was a very sensitive kid and my mother knew that I was different... or that something was 'not right' with me. Because I was different from her other children, she bullied and abused me. She also made sure that my brothers and sisters joined her in her bullying campaign... and they did, to please her.

My mother dressed me in girl's clothes and paraded me in front of her friends to show them how cute and pretty I was. This stopped when I was 5 after my father confronted her about it. When I was 8 years old, my mother took me to see a doctor, and said to the doctor: "I brought him here for you to look at his ass and tell me if there is something wrong with him, because if he is not sick, I am going to kill him."

Obviously, she did not kill me, but she made sure that I experienced true physical and psychological torture. I was 9 when my mother burnt my face with hot meat from the barbecue. Many years have passed and I still literally carry the emotional and physical scars of her abuse on my face.

Based on her mentally distorted belief — that being gay is the most terrible evil sin in the world — she kicked me out of her house when I was 12. I struggled to survive, lived in the streets, was sometimes close to starvation, and even worked as a slave just to have some food to eat.

I had my first sexual experience with a guy when I was 17 years old. I quickly developed a pattern of getting guys for sex and looking for protection from them. Once I got the protection, I lost sexual interest. Once my interest waned, the guys left, which left me heartbroken. I was trapped in this pattern for many years and only recently realised the impact it had on my life. I am working to change this.

For anyone who's not visited Brazil yet, I invite you to go and experience the world's largest and most famous street party, the Rio Carnival. The São Paulo gay pride is one of most famous gay prides in the world, with a record of 4 million participants present this year. Since the abolition of slavery in the late 19th century, the state of Bahia has become one of the most exciting places to visit. It has an exotic cultural mix of Africans, Italians, Portuguese, Lebanese, Japanese and native Indians. The cultural diversity of Brazil makes me extremely proud of where I come from.

Today, I am proud of who I am, proud of my history and my beautiful country, proud of having had the experiences of both 'heaven' and 'hell' in my life. I see my life as one that is intensely beautiful. It took me a long time, but I am happy to be gay. I still don't like being labelled as just another gay man. I don't think 'gay' is all that I am. I am also an amazing and beautiful human being who deserves and demands to be treated with as much respect as I give. I believe that wisdom is knowing that I am nothing, love is knowing that I am everything. And between the two, my life moves.

Dear Fernando,

I am sorry. I wish I could take away the pain you are going through now.

I am sorry...

I know that you are going to be okay.

How did you manage to survive everything you went through? You are a tough kid. I am proud of you.

Love,

Fernando

*"The main problem with this obsession with saving time is
very simple: you can't save time. You can only spend it. But
you can spend it wisely or foolishly."*

Benjamin Hoff

Andrew - 54

My religious parents did not allow me to befriend anyone who wasn't Catholic and since none lived in my neighbourhood, I had no friends. I was very lonely; in school, I found the other kids difficult to understand. They treated me as an outsider. I realised at a very early age that what the majority perceived as 'normal' seemed foreign and incomprehensible to me.

I believe my success in life is partially driven by these early experiences.

From my first memory, I had a burning desire to understand the world I lived in. Disappointingly, the only answers I got from my parents were bigoted religious statements. At age 8, I listed 72 things I wanted, which I randomly split into two equal groups. For many weeks, I prayed hard to receive those in one group but not the other; I received fewer in the prayed for group than the other. This proved to me, prayer does not work. From then, I stopped praying! I realised self-study and reading gave me better and more trustworthy answers than blind faith did. I began to explore deeply and widely.

This posed a problem: I knew no one else like me. None of my peers had a similar need to explore the human condition and the world we live in so intensely. At 16, almost by chance, I read my first philosophy book. I was stunned to discover that what I had been doing was exactly what the great philosophers had done throughout the ages. I was not mad, as I had thought, and I was not alone... Albert Einstein was right when he said: "The most incomprehensible thing about the universe is that it is comprehensible."

I went to university and pursued a career in IT. I worked my way from the bottom up and started my own business, which has become extremely successful and has given me great wealth. In spite of all my material riches, when asked what I needed the most after suddenly losing my partner of 27 years, there was no hesitation: to see my husband again, to hug and kiss him deeply.

I still cry when I think of him.

I have been blessed to find love again. I'm married and now share my life with an extraordinary man. Nothing compares to the wholesome joy of loving another human being.

Dear Andrew,

Know that you are a good person with great potential. Your continuous striving to understand the world around you at all levels from quantum mechanics, through psychology and social culture to astronomy, will pay off in ways you cannot now understand. It may not seem like it now, but you will be stronger, better grounded, more successful and materially better off than all those who currently surround you.

Your strategy of making decisions with your head and expressing them with your heart is a good one. When you suffer setbacks, make them lessons from which you learn. Be honest to yourself, in your deepest existential heart; from this, you will gain enormous strength.

Do not become one of the manipulated masses that unthinkingly follow leaders, adverts and celebrities. Always think for yourself. Never assume the majority are right simply because they are the majority. The Catholic crusaders, neither the Cambodian Khmer Rouge nor the German Nazis were right simply because they outnumbered others. Don't assume you have to be 'normal' — who wants to be average? Think and work out the answers yourself: "every great advancement of knowledge has involved the absolute rejection of authority" — Thomas Huxley.

Read the great philosophers of history, many have much to teach you, though others are confounded by the limitations of their age. Pay attention to Kant, and reason through the conditions and limits of reason. All wise men know they are fools, only fools think they are wise.

Communicate your truth quietly and clearly and as far as possible be on good terms with all; listen to others, take kindly the counsel of the years, but avoid loud and aggressive persons, they are irritations to the spirit. If you compare yourself with others, you may become vain and bitter, for always there will be greater and lesser persons than yourself.

Be yourself. Do not feign affection, nor be cynical about love — it is the most deeply precious thing in life. Love is simple: communicate what each other wants and if you are happy with that aim, compassionately help your partner become whatever he wishes to be. This is a mutually re-enforcing circle. There is nothing more rewarding in life than finding someone to love and having your love returned.

Life is a fleeting moment, which passes more quickly than you will ever imagine; build up your resources and sensibly enjoy them to the full. You do not get a second chance. Life is short.

Now get on with it, it's already much later than you think.

Look to this day
For it is life,
The very life of life.
In its brief course lie all
The realities and truths of existence.
The joy of growth
The splendour of action
The glory of power.

For yesterday is but a memory
And tomorrow only a vision.
But today well lived
Makes every yesterday a memory of happiness
And every tomorrow a vision of hope.
Look well to this day.

With love,

Andrew

"Be the change you want to see in the world."

Mahatma Gandhi

José - 39

I was brought up in a very strict, Catholic environment. My family went to church every Sunday and I attended a Catholic school. My mother's attitude towards sex was — and still is — extremely conservative, so sexuality — let alone homosexuality — was never discussed. In fact, my mother didn't even want me to have a girlfriend, until I finished my studies.

My father left us when I was a toddler and I had no other male role models while growing up. Whenever I asked my mother what my father was like, she only told me negative things about him. This put pressure on me to accept that he was 'a nasty piece of work'. This saddened me, which was yet another emotion, among many other negative feelings, that I bottled up.

For as long as can I remember, I've had body image issues and felt very insecure about my body. I was born without the ligament in my left heel, which left me with no control over my left foot. This made me much more reliant on my mother, in comparison to other children. For instance, I always had to hold onto her hand in public, to stop me from falling over.

I was 6 or 7 when I had an operation that gave me an artificial ligament in my left heel. This improved my walking. Afterwards, I still went for annual check-ups, because I was told that the artificial ligament would need to be replaced when I grew older. Luckily, when I reached my late teens, the doctors told me that further surgery was not necessary.

I was also born with a squint (lazy eye) and had four operations on my eyes to correct this, between the ages of 5 and 11. None of the procedures were successful, and I wore an eye patch a lot of the time.

The result of my health problems and the many operations I had was that the kids at school teased, bullied and pestered me. I became very quiet and kept to myself, because I found interacting with the other children very difficult.

I still have limited use of my left foot. Sometimes I still take a tumble but I usually manage to stay on my feet. However, occasionally I still fall, and then it's usually my ego that gets more bruised than any other part of my body.

The words 'poof', 'queer' and 'gay' were common insults on the school playground. At first, I didn't know what these words meant, but soon I realised people used them in association with something 'bad'. I knew that I was 'different' in Primary School and became consciously aware of my homosexuality during Secondary School, but as you can imagine, I was unable to discuss this with anyone.

In Primary School, I had only one friend, Fernando. We were both Portuguese and like me, Fernando was also very shy. He was also bullied, since he was partially deaf in one ear and had to wear a hearing aid. In the first year of Secondary School, we went on a school trip to France. Rather than stay in a hotel, we stayed with a French family, where we happened to share a double bed.

I can't remember how it started, but I remember being attracted to Fernando. We started, just brushing against each other, which led to touching while we were in bed. It didn't progress beyond that. At some point during the trip, I think we both became embarrassed or ashamed of what we were doing and we stopped. Nothing happened between us after that.

I unintentionally told some kid at school what happened between me and Fernando and he ran off and told everyone else. As a result, both Fernando and I were bullied for being gay. The homophobic bullying continued throughout Secondary School. Fernando and I stayed friends, but gradually we drifted apart and eventually lost contact. I know that he still lives with his parents not far from my mother's house.

My isolation as a child continued into adulthood. I find meeting other gay guys very difficult. The lack of a father figure and male role model in my life has made it difficult for me to relate to other men.

In fact, I find it hard to build relationships with men. I tend to be very quiet and shy, and I still lack the confidence to approach guys that I find attractive. I automatically assume that they won't find me attractive. I subconsciously support this 'belief' by over-eating and not looking after myself physically. Over-eating (comfort eating), especially sugary food, has also been a form of self-medication.

My relationship with my mother is as difficult as ever. As she grows older, I think that our differences are pulling us further apart. Recently, I met my father for the first time in 20 years. This was a very powerful, emotional and liberating experience which has brought me closer to a place of self-acceptance.

Though I still find myself deeply insecure and extremely self-critical when it comes to expressing my sexuality, I feel I am making progress with everything I need to overcome. As a result of my upbringing and the challenges I faced and still struggle with, I am very empathetic and caring towards others, which is why I have chosen to become a Health Coach and mental health worker. It's my way of reaching out to others, while healing my own wounds.

I am going through a phase of self-reflection now and I am beginning to be comfortable about leaving my comfort zone (something I have avoided most of my life). I intend to continue on this journey of self-discovery, wherever it may take me.

I deserve to be loved.

Dear José,

It saddens me to know that you were so lonely. But I'm glad that you had one close friend, Fernando, who was as shy as you were and shared your 'big secret'. That school trip to France with him was very eventful and I know that the yearnings and experimenting with your gay identity were both exciting and frightening.

Sadly, what was supposed to be a wonderful time of discovery in your life made you feel a lot of pain instead, especially when the other kids started bullying you, after you told them that you are gay. You are not to blame for their actions. They picked on you because they saw you as 'weak'. Weak because you had so many medical operations in Primary School and 'weak' because you are gay.

These things are all so far from the truth. Being different is not a weakness. So don't judge yourself, because you were not wrong.

Mum and Dad were dealing with their own problems and it felt as if you grew up without having any parents at all. I agree with you: they should've been there when you needed them. But Dad left home when you were still a toddler, leaving you without a father figure, or a male role model.

Life was tough on you and things were not made any easier when all you heard about Dad was negative: 'womaniser', 'wife-beater' and 'alcoholic'. You longed to know the truth about him, but one day when you find out who he really is, you will know that you are the better and stronger man.

Mum projected her depression, pain and self-hatred onto you, making you responsible for her happiness and wellbeing. As a young man, you've shown incredible strength in coping with her pain as well as your own.

I hope that one day you will learn that we are all responsible for our own happiness.

I understand why it was so difficult for you to tell anyone that you fancy men. You received so many negative messages about being gay: the bullies at school , the Catholic Church and school, the media telling the world that HIV/AIDS is a 'Gay Disease', the law and Mum wanting you to marry a 'nice Portuguese girl'.

I now know why you suppress your feelings and hide from the world. You've always tried to make yourself as 'invisible' as possible, hoping and praying that no one will notice you and bring you harm. Feeling this pain and confusion is overwhelming and scary. I feel it with you.

The irony is that the REAL you is amazing and should be seen by the world. So, reach out and talk about your feelings. Be vulnerable, because that's where your strength lies.

Believe me when I say, you are a loveable and remarkable person.

I don't have all the answers. It will be a bumpy ride, but one well worth going on. Know that you will be loved, so let other people, including other gay men, see the REAL you.

Be kind to yourself.

Lots of Love,

José

*"I am not what happened to me;
I am what I choose to become."*
Carl Jung

Christopher - 40

I was born in the north of England on the East Coast in a place called Bridlington. My mother and father separated when I was very young and I can't recall much of what happened. However, I do remember my mother being in pain and feeling depressed, both when she lived with my father and after their separation and divorce.

My father used to beat my mother and as a result she removed us from his house in fear for all our safety. We moved in with my phenomenally loving grandparents. Life became much happier. Mum fell in love with a nice guy, called Paul, who I liked even if he was odd with his long hair. Paul was really kind towards me. He often bounced me on his knee and gave me cuddles and comfort. Sadly, this was not going to last for long.

I was about 8 or 9. We had moved away from my grandparents and it was just Mum, my sister and me — life changed again... It was a beautiful sunny day. Paul pulled up in his bright red Postman Pat van. Mum came out to welcome him. The two of them exchanged harsh words and Paul drove off without saying goodbye. Back inside, Mum was upset as she explained that Paul left us because he didn't want children. This devastated my mother. I kept wondering what did I do that was so offensive that made Paul leave without saying goodbye. I felt the same abandonment when I had been separated from my grandfather, and to a lesser extent my father. I believed that everything was entirely my wrongdoing.

This feeling of abandonment and not being good enough and loveable laid the foundation for many bad experiences to come. I have memories of my father forcing me to play rugby when I visited him on compulsory custodial Sundays between 10am and 6pm. I was short, fat and weak and yet had to crawl in-between the legs of much older and larger boys when they formed the scrum. My father was determined to make a man of me... I'm not sure which hurt more, the ice covered rugby pitch against my cheek or the studded boots as the older and bigger boys trampled over me...

Entering the showers afterwards was equally terrifying... the ice cold water pelting against my skin, and the other boys noticing my embarrassment as I stood naked in front of them. This is where I felt I was different from the other boys, for the first time. I was uneasy being naked in front of them. I was rubbish at the sport and had failed to do the simplest thing for my dad. Compared to the other boys I was hopeless and a wimp.

At home with my mother, I felt equally out of place. My sister was the complete opposite to me, tall, with beautiful long dark hair and deep brown eyes. She was most comfortable rebelling against everyone and everything and got attention by acting up. She soon became the black sheep of the family, whereas I was 'the good boy' with my blond hair and blue eyes; being the cute, quiet and dutiful son who desperately wanted to be loved. If my sister and I were chess pieces, I'd be the white set with mother, and my sister would be the black set teaming up with my father. This chess game was blindingly obvious, with my father using my sister — who was his favourite child — as his force of hatred against me or mother. In turn, my sister made sure I knew how worthless I was. She called me a girl, which really distressed me. She even forced me to wear girl's clothes and makeup at times.

At school, I didn't find the kids warm and friendly either. During school PE we would be forced to canoe out into the cold sea. The other boys would terrorise me by making me believe they'd capsize my boat, or actually doing it. I was a weak swimmer and wore thick glasses that looked like the glass bottoms of milk bottles. I might as well have worn a sign saying, 'Pick on me!'. I became the target of torment for the other boys, who called me names like 'specky four eyes' at best. Other names soon followed, like bummer, fudge packer, arse bandit, shirt lifter.

In order to escape this misery I created a whole fantasy world of my own. Malcolm and Alan, identical twins who worked for British Rail, befriended me. With them, I fitted in. My desire to belong somewhere was so strong that I 'converted' my old black school blazer by fixing British Rail logos to the lapels. Malcolm and Alan got me a porter's hat from the stores department. Wearing my makeshift uniform I used to sweep platforms, clean trains and clip tickets... passengers genuinely believed I was an apprentice working on the railway. This was my sanctuary and where I felt comfortable and at one in the world.

I had two friends at school and we experimented with sexual games among ourselves. We'd play strip/dare poker. It was very exciting to watch my friend intentionally play so badly that he'd have to strip down, slowly exposing his smooth, fresh, white skin. We'd both be aroused and have erections. Once naked we'd dare each other to rub up against one another, gradually getting bolder and bolder with our dares and acts. However, I don't recall having penetrative sex until I was aged 18 or 19.

Aged 13, I decided to no longer see my father. It was around the same time that I became aware of being 'different' — liking boys and not girls. My grandfather had always been a stable father figure in my life and when it became too much to live with mother, I stayed with him and my grandmother. Granddad was an ex-World War soldier and I couldn't imagine him accepting me the way that I am. I was certain that I would shame him, and that he would be unable to love me. Still to this day I don't know what happened. I don't know if I backed away from him, or him me. Either way, aged 13, I lost the intimacy and warmth from the man I truly regarded as my father.

At 16, I left school with no qualifications. I desperately wanted to run away and needed to find my happiness somewhere else. However, moving away also served as punishment to my mother and just as I had done with my father, I planned to never speak to her or see her again. I moved in with my great-aunt and uncle in Sandbanks, a beautiful and much sought-after neighbourhood of Bournemouth. My aunt taught me how to speak 'proper' English, in order to succeed in life. With her encouragement, I became more self-assured and still today, people think I have had private education and ooze self-confidence.

I first came 'out' to my best friend, Sarah, whom I had met doing volunteer work. I plucked up the courage after drinking a whole bottle of vodka. It wasn't a pleasant experience and I suffered with alcohol poisoning for a few days after. Sarah and Jane, another nurse we volunteered with, continued to love me despite being gay. It was such a relief.

I finally found the confidence to visit a gay night club for the first time, when I was almost 20. I went home with a guy that evening and we had sex. This was during the late 80s and early 90s and AIDS was seen as a 'gay man's disease'. I did not have the confidence to tell the guy to wear a condom. I was passive; it was painful and I did not enjoy it. The whole experience reinforced in my mind that gay sex was disgusting, degrading, painful, and dangerous. It was an experience I did not want to repeat for a long time. However, my need for love and acceptance eventually would override my fears... I had learnt my lesson though: from here on I'd practice safer sex.

My financial situation, coupled with the sudden and tragic death of my sister's husband, meant that I moved back to Yorkshire and stayed with my sister. During the next couple of years we talked about our childhood and realised that we both went through the same traumatic experiences. The bond we made during this time has remained unbroken since.

Both my sister and I sought comfort in the church. My sister for the loss of her husband, and I wanted to recreate God's fatherly love which had been taught during Sunday School. As a child and until my late teens I believed I had a calling to become a Vicar and do God's work. However, being much older and more aware of my own urges and feelings, I fell in love with my best friend at church. I told the Vicar that I was gay, who told me that my best friend had similar 'tendencies'. The Vicar reviewed the scripture with me but didn't focus so much on God's unconditional love. Instead, he highlighted that according to the Bible, I could never inherit the Kingdom of God as a practicing homosexual. Apparently, in the eyes of the church, I was an abomination.

I was convinced to pray to God for Him to change me. I gave God a commitment and abstained from sex for a year. At the end of that year, I was still the same person, even though the church had allegedly cast out my homosexuality. However, as the Vicar yet again prayed over me, something was cast away indeed. I cried and literally fell to my knees as I realised that according to the evangelical church God did not love me just as I am... in fact He rejected my entire being. I left that church knowing that God had not changed me and that being gay wasn't important to God.

At the age of 20, I had built bridges with all family relationships except that with my father. I fell in love for the first time and moved in with my first boyfriend. He was ten years older than me and a stable influence in my life. We set up our own business, which was relatively successful. As I gained confidence, I came out to my mother and grandmother. The more I gained confidence the more I wanted to explore being gay and sleeping around. The stability my older partner once gave me, I now found boring and restrictive. I was never really happy living in Yorkshire and yearned to move back to Bournemouth, and start again. At 22, this is exactly what I did.

I used my mask of confidence to over-state my qualifications and experience. I had the title 'Financial Controller' on my CV and this would now open many doors in the future. I met the love of my life, Craig, shortly after arriving in Bournemouth. It was the summer holidays; bright and sunny days just like my early child-hood memories of Bournemouth. Life was good. However, Craig was at university in London and went back in September, once summer was over.

That December, when he returned on my birthday and broke up with me, I was devastated. However, I had a good circle of friends and earned good money for someone with no formal qualifications. I still visited Craig in London and he introduced me to the club scene and we took our first Ecstasy — the dance drug — together. Everything was just so fabulous and I honestly thought that being gay was fantastic. Taking Ecstasy meant I could dance for the first time without feeling awkward. For the first time in my life I could let myself go and express myself. The misery of my childhood and teens was surely forgotten. This is what life was about, I had arrived.

In my career I reached a glass ceiling by only being qualified by experience. If I wanted to play with the big boys, I'd have to address my education. So far, I had managed to deceive my employers by dressing the part and looking like a well-groomed successful businessman. I did not correct any assumptions about my education unless directly asked. The auditor in my first senior role, a very kind and good Muslim man, recognised my potential and encouraged me to start night school.

Four years later, I passed my professional qualifications in accountancy. For me, this was a great accomplishment: the boy who suffered with dyslexia passing and becoming a professional accountant. So, I pushed myself harder. Unless I was killing myself in work I viewed myself as lazy and incompetent. I aimed to avoid the feeling of failure at any cost and started to even sacrifice myself. I formed an unhealthy relationship of gaining self-worth from career status, material objects and money.

My childhood mantra of being fat and ugly has continued throughout my 20s and 30s, and to a degree today at age 40, I still partially believe this is true. Still unable to create my own positive feelings toward myself, I would look to others to provide this. A night out would not be successful unless I went home with someone who completely validated me on a physical level. I loved the drugs and the dancing, which gave so much confidence. I would isolate myself in my own little dancing world at the front of the stage. People would look up at me and smile, wave and laugh. I could pick anyone from the crowd... Sadly sometimes, I would pick guys up only to relieve my sexual frustration, and in turn affirm exactly how I felt about myself.

I was an outstanding employee. The more responsible my position, the higher the salary, the higher the salary the more I'd be compelled to perform. I still believed I was a fraud and my fear of being discovered drove me to work harder. Yet my fear was unfounded because I completely neglected to look at the real facts: I succeeded in my first two jobs, despite lying about my qualifications. I was now a professional accountant, who was paid the market rate for a European Finance Director, I spoke sense in the boardroom, was fantastic at motivating teams and gained an unbelievable amount of respect from peers. My CV, for ten or more years, accurately portrayed my work experience and job title and responsibilities. Still, in my mind, I was a fraud.

I stayed at work for even longer and exhausted myself and I gave no emotional support to my partner. I took more drugs and eventually could not have sex without using. While on drugs, I could have sex for hours, days, and long weekends... and I did. I now became aware that I was good-looking, and for as long as I had drugs I could pull this off in bed too. Drugs took away the edge of not having any real self-confidence and created a strong sense of love and intimacy. At any other time I could only express my love by being the provider of accommodation, food, money and holidays, and drugs allowed me to relax enough to be intimate and emotionally close. In order to feel loved, unless on drugs, I'd need material things in return. Nothing less than high brand and expensive.

Life was good.

I had totally bought in to the work hard and play hard gay life style. Spending money and running up massive credit lines was a way of validating how successful I was, and therefore my perception of acceptability from society. I was now into six sum salaries, a £750,000 house, travelled first class around the world on luxury 5-star holidays. Nothing but the best would do. I owned so many computers and gadgets and had to have every new Gay App on every device. I could have whatever I wanted. Money lost its true value.

About five years ago, I hit what I perceive as a 'milestone' in my life. I had seen it coming as the company I worked for went through an acquisition by a global organisation. I was made redundant and rewarded handsomely. I received my annual salary as a severance package and as a 'thank you' for doing such an outstanding job, yet all I could feel was the rejection of my childhood. My boyfriend at the time was emotionally unavailable and could not support me during this time. On top of losing my job, his rejection was too much to deal with, and my self-worth was now in tatters.

My sexual conduct was now spiralling into being harmful and destructive along with my cocaine use. Within a few days, I had a couple of low risk unprotected sex encounters and shortly after I became so ill, I actually thought I was dying. I joined the dots between feeling ill and having unprotected sex. It crossed my mind that I might have contracted HIV. However, with everything else going on in my life, I did not have the emotional bandwidth to deal with this.I escaped by watching porn and taking harmful amounts of coke. I saw my dealer every day, or every other day. I'd spend hours on gay dating sites, filling the long summer's day with an endless search for a connection with someone who wouldn't reject me.

It was one of the wettest summers on record in the UK so I booked a ticket and went off to travel Mexico and the USA for several months. I didn't want to feel the rejection I felt after losing my job, and neither did I want to be reminded of the bronchitis I had a few weeks earlier, so I substituted cocaine for alcohol. I guess taking mind-altering substances and abusing alcohol numbed me completely and I uncharacteristically saw little reason in wearing protection whenever I had sex. My self-worth was so low that I really didn't care if I died. If I really fancied the guy, and I was drunk, I wanted to feel as intimate as possible with him. My reasoning was that since my last HIV test was negative and even if in the unlikely event I was HIV positive, he probably was... otherwise he'd surely say no to having unprotected sex.

I fell in love with a beautiful man whilst overseas but these were uncharted waters. I discovered a song by Mika, called *Any Other World* with the lyrics *"Say goodbye to the world you thought you lived in..."* I never practised unprotected sex unless in a relationship and not before three months, and only then after confirming both of us had a negative status. I got tested and the result returned positive. In future I'd wear a condom to protect my partner and not my safety... Life changed again.

Being HIV positive immediately tapped into another childhood mantra: "I am dirty", "I am disgusting", "I am broken" and "I am unloveable". I gave up alcohol and cocaine for about six months in an effort to be more healthy. I fell in love with a guy who was HIV negative — at least I wouldn't be coping on my own with all these feelings. However, I was so ashamed of my infection that it complicated our sex life. Despite always being safe, he broke up with me every four to six months as he processed his fears of being in a relationship with someone who was infected. Not having a healthy sexual relationship meant I'd self-medicate feelings of rejection and being dirty by using huge quantities of cocaine.

I followed my habitual pattern of being ambiguous in relationships, and once we had overcome the fact that I was positive, I lost interest in him. Our relationship ended. As much as we loved each other, I now know the basis of this relationship was very unhealthy. I found a gay dating website predominately for guys with HIV and the doors opened for me to have sex with loads of gorgeous guys. I thought as we had all gone through the trauma of being diagnosed positive, this would be the perfect place to find a boyfriend.

In this world of very good looking men, practicing unsafe sex without the fear of killing each other, I enjoyed being intimate again. However, much as this was liberating, I was also introduced to the drug Crystal Meth — Methamphetamine. I knew the substance was highly addictive but since I had once given up cocaine when I needed to, I thought I was mentally strong enough not to become an addict... I'd walk away before it became a problem.

I went missing in action for three days the second time I took the drug and didn't bother to phone in sick to work... not acceptable behaviour for a European Finance Director. I got fired. The pain of falling short of the standards I had set for myself was great. I had broken almost every promise I made to myself and the people in my life who loved me: I had cheated on my partners, got HIV and infected other guys while I didn't know that I was positive. I couldn't live with my emotions and had so much to hide from. I escaped by using Crystal Meth and sex, I played with both very hard.

After the six weeks I decided to return to reality and start looking for a job. I stopped having sex and stopped taking Crystal... In less than six hours I had a migraine and severe flu, I was shaking, I felt dreadful. It quickly dawned on me that I was suffering from withdrawal symptoms. I immediately rang my dealer to fix the 'problem'. I actually took pleasure in rebelling against everything I had once stood for. Yet still, I went to rehab but I was unco-operative and in too much pain. I was released and carried on with my drug abuse. Fortunately, they taught me a new mantra in rehab: "Nothing changes if nothing changes". For six months, I carried on behaving destructively. But the problem with using mind-altering substances over a sustained period of time is they are like steroids for the mind, and they alter one's mind. Of course, I did not notice these changes.

I became paranoid and placed myself in dangerous situations. The police and ambulance service became frequent callers at my front door. On at least four occasions, I was detained and held under the Mental Health Act, and assessed for sectioning. I was never committed because I knew how to wangle myself out of this. I did not want help. Eventually I made several attempts to end my life.

Nothing changes if nothing changes. 18 months ago, I joined Narcotics Anonymous (NA - the Alcoholics Anonymous for drug users) and have made many new true friends since — people who share my desire to stop their destructive and addictive behaviours. The struggle to overcome addiction has been the most difficult challenge in my entire life. I remember the quote "What doesn't kill us, makes us stronger" and this has proven to be true, both in my HIV diagnosis and in the more deathly disease of addiction.

To think all of this stemmed from something so simple as taking Ecstasy. The progressive nature of drug addiction in someone who is prone to having a lack of self-worth should not be underestimated. I am saddened when I reflect on my life, especially the past five years, and I realise the destruction I caused in my own and so many other lives, all because I was simply searching for myself, to feel authentic self-worth and stop believing all those negative things I told myself from a very early age. I now realise my addiction and desire to externally fix my life is the result of the trauma of growing up gay in a straight world.

The medical profession would probably tell me I was conditioned for addiction as a result of my childhood. They are probably right, but through NA, I have been taught that I am the result of how I reacted to what happened to me as a child. My loving NA friends now show me how to approach life following a simple programme which breaks my habitual patterns of reaction and calamity. I have searched for myself for 40 years and I can honestly say that today I have found inner peace.

Nothing changes if nothing changes: my mantra today, in most instances, is I am an amazingly wonderful loving and powerful man with extraordinary life experiences.

So long as I follow my recovery programme, just for today I shall be enough just as I am.

If you are reading my story and you're concerned about your own sex, drink or drug use. or you feel things are becoming a little unmanageable, please seek help.

"Never lose hope because hope is beautiful."

Dear Christopher,

I know you think you know everything, but I ask that you read this letter with an open mind.

The journey we are about to embark on is going to be quite extraordinary, exciting and rewarding. Yet the irony is that at the age of 40 you will return to a similar place emotionally than where you are right now: the good, the excitement, the possibilities and leaving unhappiness behind... but also the bad and the searching questions: Who am I? What are my values? Am I enough? Am I loveable?

I know you believe nobody loves or likes you and that you never will fit in. You believe moving to Bournemouth — running away — will solve your problems. I can tell you now, there is no escaping one's problems and there are no external places that will bring the peace, love and acceptance you're looking for. You can never successfully run away from yourself.

Despite all of this, you will become quite an amazing person. However, you won't achieve all of this on your own and you have to abandon the belief that you can do everything by yourself...

You'll also find that the more genuine you are, instead of being how you think others want you to be, the more love you'll receive from your friends and family. This love and acceptance will become something you will heavily rely on and value.

Finally, I want to say sorry and please forgive me for the places I will take you to. In my defence, I became lost and completely disorientated and as a result, I abandoned you the same way Mum and Dad had done.

Never give up. Trust the process. You can become whatever you want to be... Or put in a different way: we become whatever we think.

Love,

Chris

APPLE-CINNAMON TEA:
MONDAY 3:30AM
Francois Lubbe

That's something I don't have —
an umbrella.
My boyfriend lost his
and the guy sitting across
the table can't whistle
or shout
but he can speak though.

Last year, I was twenty
but I've come a lot further than most
twenty-year-olds, or so I'm told.
Someone sings about his best
that wasn't good enough
and I wonder about my own…

We have another cup of tea
and drip and drab
in and out of conversation,
when all we really want to say is:

Please hold us.
We are young and can get hurt too.
Don't give us umbrellas and words —
they won't protect us from life
and its teachings...
(don't chase us away from what we are feeling)

CHAPTER TWO

DEVELOPING LIMITING BELIEFS

As human beings, we have an inborn drive to find meaning in our lives and to understand why things are the way they are. That's why young children always inquisitively ask 'why?' followed by 'but why?' and then another 'why?' again. For this reason, the young gay child, who perceives himself to be oddly out of place, will start to look for a meaning and reason for him being different. Without the proper guidance and support from a mentor or a parent, chances are good that he will start to develop certain limiting beliefs about himself.

In the previous chapter, we saw how feeling oddly out of place surfaced in our lives in many different ways. Some of us noticed that we did not enjoy the games most of the other boys liked to play. Others preferred to hang out with the girls in the playground instead of being part of a gang or a football team. Some of us preferred to spend more time with our mothers, while our fathers gradually faded into the background and some of us simply did not notice any obvious signs of being different; we just knew that we were not like the other boys.

Yet few gay men can remember that anyone ever noticed how they felt or said to them 'you are okay exactly as you are'. It sounds like very simple words, but this positive affirmation and validation is something gay men rarely experience as they grow up. Instead, many of us remember the exact opposite — being constantly invalidated by our families, friends and peers. Some of us were teased and called names at school, at home and everywhere in between. For others, life was and still is much tougher.

Recent research from the UK charity Stonewall indicates that homophobic bullying is still rampant in UK schools. The charity Diversity Role Models estimates that lesbian, gay, bisexual and transgender (LGBT) young people are three times more likely to attempt suicide. This harsh reality was recently echoed in a news article by a gay journalist who wrote, "For four years, high school became my own private hell. A nightmarish, David-and-Goliath-type war, fought daily on a public battlefield. My battle scars run deep. You just can't see them."

On a positive note, some gay charities and organisations say that things are changing for the better. An example being the 'It Gets Better Project' that was founded in the United States in response to the suicides of teenagers who were bullied because they were gay or because their peers perceived them to be gay. 'It Gets Better' promotes the message that now is the best time ever in history to be young and gay. This certainly is a hopeful message, and in some instances, the evidence suggests that things are indeed changing for the better. However, there is still a long way to go regardless of statistics. Homophobic bullying is very much a reality for many gay children and lays the foundation for many self-defeating behaviours and limiting beliefs.

Even though we've enjoyed more media exposure in recent years, there are still few positive images of diverse gay role models in magazines, films and on television. The negative portrayal of homosexuality in the past still has an impact on how the gay community is seen today. As a result, many gay men grow up with a negative stereotypical image of what being gay means. For instance, enter any gay bar in the world and you'll find a strategically placed display table, stacked with magazines that portray gay men as sexy, wild, party animals. These images perpetuate the mainstream's perception that gay men are shallow and superficial which not only deceives Joe Public, but also the countless young and impressionable gay teenagers who are struggling to find a sense of identity. Even though these over-sexualised images are tantalizing and alluring, they send messages that can trigger limiting beliefs that tell us that we have to be beautiful in order to be accepted or that if we have a perfect body, we'll finally find love and a place to belong.

It's only in recent years that gay and mainstream media have started to depict a more balanced and less racy image of gay life and it's refreshing to see that the focus is shifting towards promoting more positive gay role models. In the past, in film and television, the stereotypical camp gay man has featured all too often whenever a gay character was portrayed on screen. This is hardly an adequate representation of the gay population. However, gay-themed films which portray gay men as balanced human beings are slowly but surely entering the mainstream. These films offer a point of view that will not only comfort many gay teenagers, but also serve as an affirmation that there is a place in the world for them.

Without the message of validation, and without well-rounded and positive role models, young gay children will continue to look for the reason for them being oddly out of place. They will keep asking 'Why don't I fit in?' and 'Why am I not accepted the way that I am?' The vicious cycle of internalising their doubts and fears and the sense of not belonging will continue, and they will almost always come to the same conclusion: 'Not fitting in or not being accepted exactly as I am has everything to do with me, and nothing to do with the world around me'. This ultimately leads to the belief that 'there is something wrong with me' and 'I am unlovable because of how I am'.

The stories shared in *Developing Limiting Beliefs* show how individual experiences and circumstances can easily lead to cultivating limiting beliefs that range from 'I am not good enough', 'I am not worthy', 'I am unloveable', 'I am a mistake' to 'I am bad'. As adults, many gay men unconsciously take these beliefs as being the truth; after all, the beliefs have been there for such a long time that it can be difficult to differentiate the facts from fiction.

Our limiting beliefs show up in our adult lives in many ways and often manifest themselves in situations where we are triggered by a set of circumstances or a single event that take us back to our childhood. For example, we make a mistake at work and instead of simply brushing it off as a human error, we tell ourselves that 'I am clearly not good enough'. Or when a relationship ends, rather than acknowledging that it just did not work out, we tell ourselves that 'I am clearly unloveable'. We continue to internalise our doubts, fears, and sense of not belonging which started in our early childhood. However, the intensity with which we feel these emotions as an adult can be so strong and so exposing that we often reach for cover or lash out at the person who triggered those feelings.

It is important to acknowledge that along with our limiting beliefs, we also develop enhancing beliefs and survival strategies to help us cope. Much as we tell ourselves that we are not good enough, unloveable or a mistake, we also tell ourselves that if we work harder, earn more money and excel in our careers, we will finally be acceptable in the eyes of the world. Ultimately, we convince ourselves that we need to behave in a certain way in order to survive and to escape any form of pain and rejection. The sad fact is that holding onto our negative beliefs which are extremely powerful can lead to depression, alcohol and substance abuse, low self-esteem and in some cases, suicide.

Once developed, these beliefs stay alive and become the fuel that runs our lives through childhood, adolescence and well into adulthood.

The impact of these limiting beliefs is evident in all the stories that follow. For some of these men, their beliefs manifested as a deep-rooted shame for being gay or a feeling of guilt after being intimate with a man. For others, it was a feeling of unworthiness and feeling abandoned and rejected. Regardless of their individual experiences, the golden thread that weaves itself through all these stories is the limiting belief that 'There is something wrong with me'.

"My mission in life is not merely to survive,
but to thrive; and to do so with some passion,
some compassion, some humour,
and some style."

Maya Angelou

Ade - 44

Some days it feels just like yesterday when I boarded a late night Nigerian Airways flight from Lagos to London. It was January 1988. I was 19 and all I thought about, as I stared out of the airplane window, was: "At last, I can finally start being me. I can finally start living my own life".

What I did not anticipate back then, was that I carried a huge amount of shame about being gay. Leaving home had not taken away my pain; it had simply travelled with me. It would take me another eight years, before I experienced my first sexual encounter with a man. Until then, I simply denied the 'gay part' of me by taking refuge in daydreams and in a church, where on most Sundays, the pastor condemned gay people. When I finally left the church, I embarked on searching for 'the one', which sadly only led to one-night stands and 'short-term' encounters. I excelled in my career, travelled continuously and found many other outlets to help numb my pain.

In 2009, I realised that I was living on the surface of my life. I was wearing a series of masks and felt disconnected from my core being. I was compromising myself and over-compensating on so many levels and was deeply dissatisfied with everything. The time had come for me to fully step into my life and to be the best version of myself — to be more congruent and authentic in my day-to-day living.

As part of embracing my true self, I visited Nigeria the following year. It was my third trip back, since I left in 1988. During this trip, I came out to mother all over again. I had done this once before in 1996, and we had never spoken about it again. It was as if the conversation had never happened.

Coming out for the second time, was much more dramatic than the first time. As the pain from the past resurfaced, my mother expressed her disappointment, sadness and shame for having a gay son. In that moment, I had a breakthrough: I had come such a long way in my own emotional journey. I was finally comfortable with being gay, regardless of whether my mother accepted me or not. I realised that 'I fully accepted myself, exactly as I am.' This realisation meant that I chose to no longer put myself in situations where I was emotionally or mentally abused — a pattern I had replicated many times since I left Nigeria.

Shortly after that conversation with my mother, I stopped communicating with her. I told her of my intention, explaining that I had reached a place in my life where I had decided that I wanted to be around people who nurtured and encouraged me. I wanted to be around people who accepted me, exactly as I am. It was the toughest decision I have had to make.

Through the years, my mother and I had been through so much together and yet somehow we had reached a place where I deeply felt that in order to step into my authentic self, I needed to let go of our relationship. I had come to realise that it was not fair on her for me to want her to change and be the person that I longed her to be, and it was not fair on me that she wanted me to be someone other than myself.

We spoke a few months after my decision to cease communication with her, she apologised for what she had said and asked for forgiveness. I accepted the apology and explained that I still stood by my decision. I felt bruised from the pain of my past and had reached a place where I did not feel emotionally safe in her presence. I had often left our encounters feeling that I had let her down for being gay, for bringing shame on her and the family. Her words and behaviour would often confirm my feelings, and each time I would hope that it be different, but it never was. I had no doubt that she loved me in her own way, but all too often this had not translated into healthy and nurturing behaviour. In June 2012, a year and half since our last contact, my mother sent me a text message. Once again, she asked for forgiveness for what she had said. She said that she missed me. I never responded…. She passed away the following month.

My relationship with my mother, like life, was a complex one. Through her, I learnt that life is about navigating those complexities. That heated conversation with her finally taught me that she deeply struggled with the fact that her only child was gay, and felt that my sexuality was something I should hide and that she felt ashamed. Whilst I understood that her opinion and beliefs were largely influenced by culture, I also knew that this was her 'story' and 'truth', and not mine. I finally know that I am okay, and that there is nothing wrong with me being gay.

My mother, albeit indirectly, taught me the importance of showing up in my own life and living my own truth. She was an amazing teacher and even though we never got round to having that final embrace, I am forever grateful that I had the opportunity to show up as myself in our relationship.

Dear Wale,

I know you keep wondering why the Valium tablets you took from your mum's handbag did not send you to sleep forever. You keep hoping for another oppor-tunity to search her bag again for some more. You feel that you have reached the end of the road and you want it all to end. Every night, just before you fall asleep, you silently pray that God must take you away from this world. Yet, each morning when you wake, you find you are still here. You wonder how you are going to make it through another day full of anger, sadness and loneliness. Yet, somehow you pull through, taking refuge in day-dreaming about a future where you are loved, seen and accepted exactly as you are. I know about all of this.

I also know that as you struggle through each day, you hope that a miracle will take you away from what you call the 'house of pain.' There are reasons for this Wale and I understand them: I know you remember being fostered from a very young age when you were in London. I fully realize the impact it had on you: living with another family from when you were only 8 weeks old, and to then be abruptly taken away from this new family, whom you had grown to love; moving back to Nigeria, when you were 6 years old.

Of course, all of this unsettled you and left you with feelings of abandonment. It is no surprise that you never felt at home with your biological parents in Nigeria, or in the land of your ancestors.

I'm sorry that you have no one to talk to about this trauma and no one sees the pain in your eyes. I am sorry that you now feel a need to pretend that you are not in pain — an attitude of being strong and reliable, and pleasing everyone, whilst distracting them from your pain. I want you to know that I recognise your pain, and that I am here for you.

I know that you feel no one sees you and that you are unloveable but I want you to hang in there for a little longer. I know that you want to leave now but before you know it, you will leave home and head back to London. Even though the next three years will feel very long, somehow you will get through it. During this time you will learn the importance of being patient and delaying gratification — lessons that will come in handy, many years from now.

That conversation you heard your parents having, late one evening, when you were 14, keeps replaying itself in your head. It makes you feel that your parents do not love you. You heard your mum ask your dad why he did not like you. As you lay in bed that night, you hoped that he would say: 'That's not true, I really love my son.'

Instead, you heard him reply: 'I'll tell you why I don't like him. In fact, there are three reasons why I don't like him. First, he does not have any hair. Second, he is not intelligent. And third he is always ill." I remember you cried yourself to sleep that night. Once again, you hoped that you wouldn't wake up the next morning.

Yes, I still hear that conversation in my head too. The pain of hearing your own father utter those words might never go away, but I now know that it had nothing to do with you. It says much more about him and where he was at with his own life at that point.

I remember that poem you wrote a few years back, which you had titled 'nobody loves me, why'. At school, all you can think about are the boys who torment you about not having hair and calling you names. You have now been wearing a cap for five years and have never taken it off in public.

I know you are ashamed about being different and standing out. A number of the kids at school tease you about the cap and the bigger boys sometimes grab it off your head and run away with it. The bullying has been going on through High School and you have not spoken to anyone about it. You simply pretend that it doesn't matter and that their words or behaviour don't hurt you.

You've also been cutting class during your final year in High School, because it's too painful to go there. You wake up in the morning and get ready for school and when you see your parents have left for work, you go back home and spend the day in front of the TV. Your grades are starting to betray your secret and you are worried about your GCE 'O'-Level results. I know you are dreading where life will take you after High School. I know about all these things too and I know that you keep praying that before long, you will leave this place.

You've known for four years now that you are attracted to boys. You keep hoping that it is just a phase and that those feelings will pass. You feel that life is challenging and painful enough, and wonder what you have done in a previous life to deserve the punishment of being this different. You feel there is no one out there who is like you and you feel so alone.

Wale, you are not alone. You will meet many other people who are gay too, just like you. Some will embrace you and some will break your heart. Don't worry, you are strong and you will be able to handle it. You will be fine. You will fall in love and you will also get to know and experience someone loving you right back. I read somewhere that 'life does not give us more than we are able to handle' and that 'the best students get the hardest tests'. So I guess you must be a pretty good 'student of life'.

The day will come when you will tell your mum that you are gay. This is hard to believe right now, but yes, you will. Regardless of how she reacts to this, I want you to know that the reason you will tell her is to show her your authentic self. You will become tired of pretending to be someone you are not.

You will not get the opportunity to come out to your dad. Sadly, he will no longer be here ten years from now. He will attempt to reconnect with you, after you leave Nigeria, and he will try to show in his own way that he does love you. I hope you have the courage to open up and let him in. If you don't, that's fine too and don't beat yourself up about it. Maya Angelou says, 'when we know better, we do better'.

I want you to know that you have YOU. This might not sound like a lot, but it's really important to know that the real YOU is your most powerful advocate. Don't bury him away, otherwise you are going to spend a long time looking for him in all the wrong places — in boyfriends, jobs, travel, clothes, money and other irrelevant things. You will not find him out there; that might not make sense right now, but it will someday.

I know that you feel that life has never given you what you have always longed for — to be loved and accepted exactly as you are. Please know that you are, and will be, loved exactly as you are; not just by me, but also by many people that you are still yet to meet and some that you already know.

You push people away, because you feel that they will reject you once they get to know the real YOU. Learn to trust again and let people in. If someone does not accept you, that's fine and it's their problem. I accept you and I want you to know this: you are loved by me. You have not been forgotten by Life. You are not inadequate, flawed, broken or damaged, and you don't need fixing. There is nothing wrong with you and you are not a mistake.

Forever yours and with all my love,
Ade(wale)

P.S. You dropped the 'Wale' from your name after you left Nigeria. You wanted it to signify leaving the past behind. However, we never leave the past behind. We can release the pain of the past and learn from its wisdom, but we never leave it behind. Remember this, and don't make attempts to pretend that the past never happened. It will only prolong the pain and suffering. I had to learn this the hard way!

*"If I speak in the tongues of men
and of angels,
but have not LOVE,
I am only a resounding gong
or a clanging cymbal.
If I have the gift of prophecy
and can fathom all mysteries
and all knowledge,
and if I have a faith
that can move mountains,
but have not LOVE,
I am nothing.
If I give all I possess to the poor
and surrender my body to the flames,
but have not LOVE,
I gain nothing."*

1 Corinthians 13

Ian - 55

From the outside, one could say that I was a happy child and teenager. I came from a good home: not wealthy, but comfortable enough. My parents were loving and caring. They wanted the best for my younger brother and myself. I was a 'good boy' and did well at school, in my 'O' and 'A' Levels. However, deep inside, I was far from happy.

At the age of two and a half, after the birth of my brother, I mistakenly believed that my mother abandoned me in favour of the new-born. Since then, I have thought of myself as being alone, separate and essentially different from others. This loneliness made me believe that, since I did not fit in, something must be wrong with me. Through my eyes, it felt that I had been rejected by my mother.

My father was somewhat absent, physically and emotionally. In fact, the truth is that I rejected both my parents (and myself). Rather than owning up to this, I have turned it around and put the blame on them. I have been replaying this scenario over and over again throughout my life.

Realising that something was 'going on' with me, my mother tried to 'fix' me by urging me to be more like my brother: confident, extroverted, good with people and so on. But this only reinforced the idea that I was not acceptable as I was. It also intensified my sense of competition and failure.

However, I now know that my mother had her hands full with coping with my newly born brother, and that I incorrectly construed her behaviour as rejection.

Questions around sexuality arose in my teenage years and I largely pushed these aside, though I could not entirely deny them (however hard I tried). They served to compound my secret fear that I was different and flawed.

As an adult, I have excelled in my career, travelled the world, founded a charity and recently became a published author. However, I still struggle to believe in my ability to have loving, caring and intimate relationships. I constantly relive the moment of fear when, as a child, I believed that something was going on between my mother and brother – something I was not a part of. This reinforces my feelings of being separate and left out.

My big issues are all still centred around abandonment or rejection, and competition or jealousy, though I've moved on a long way through a process of self-acceptance (not to be confused with self-improvement). This has mostly come about with the aid of a profound spiritual book called *A Course in Miracles*. Through the teachings and lessons it contains, I am learning that I am perfect and loveable just the way I am. I wish I had known as a child, what I know now about myself.

Dear Ian,

I know that you are in a very painful place right now, and that you are confused about who and what you are. All you know is that you feel you don't belong. For years, you have felt like an alien in your own life. You crave connection with your family and with others, but don't feel connected.

You ask yourself: "Who are these people I live with? I'm not one of them. I don't belong here." You do not realise that this is a decision that you have made, the result of which is that you have withdrawn into angry self-reliance — telling yourself that you don't need other people. What you don't realise is that you made a mistake and you rejected them — just as you are continuing to do with people today.

I want you to know that the way things are simply need not be. Just reach out to people and connect. Reach out, not in need, but in celebration of being alive and being human.

If you choose to do this, it will be rewarded, many times over, with others reaching out to you, embracing, holding and loving you. Everyone wants to connect with others too. If you withdraw, you will feel disconnected, as you have always done. I encourage you to be more proactive and make it a conscious choice to move towards people, rather than hide away in your own little world of study, solo hobbies and... things.

You cannot have relationships with rocks, stamps and old records. You need people. And they need you!

The truth is that you are perfect and loveable, just as you are, even though you don't believe that. All you have to do is to connect with that part of yourself that knows this about you. It is the truth.

How people respond to you is up to them and has nothing whatsoever to do with you. It means nothing about you, despite what you think. People have their own issues to deal with, which bear no reflection on you.

Connect and feel connected, regardless. What you give, you receive. Come from a place of wholeness and completion and see the results mirrored back to you by other people. Seek not to be liked, but seek to like others, as best you can. When you see and know the truth in them, you will see it and know it in yourself.

I love you, Ian, and I want you to know that you are loveable. Nothing is wrong or not exactly as it should be. You are perfect now! Celebrate and love that!

Love yourself,

Ian

"All I want of you, Men and Women
Is that you shall achieve your own beauty
As the flowers do."

D.H. Lawrence

Paul - 45

In many ways, although I struggled with a sense of 'not being good enough' from a very age in my life, it was also a driving force in my life to help others. Once I came to the conclusion that there was nothing 'wrong' with being gay and by accepting myself, taking the leap from being straight to being gay was not that daunting. I left gay shame for gay pride! I faced a prejudiced world and took a stand against the erroneous equation that homosexuals are not equal to other human beings. This injustice still fills me with righteous anger.

Anger at discrimination can be a great thing and it can help exact change in the world. It certainly helped me to find my voice and I took part in many wonderful marches and demonstrations, where I stood united with many beautiful gay activist friends. One can say I almost became a professional protester! I marched for Gay Pride, Anti-Clause 28 (an intolerant and unjust law marginalising gay people in the UK), Antiapartheid in South Africa and even the UK's 1984-85 Miners' Strike.

These marches were all worthy and exciting events to be a part of. I recognized that while the wheels of 'oppression' have turned for me as a gay man, others caught up in the same machinery deserved equal compassion, understanding and outrage. However, despite my outward fury and provocative actions advocating GAY PRIDE, I was still suffering from a crippling lack of self-worth... The burden of shame and self-loathing was still there... In retrospect, I wish I showed the same courage to stand up for myself that I've shown in standing up for others.

I have always been deeply compassionate to the needs of others, but learned that, at times, this was a smokescreen for not taking care of myself. As a result, I have allowed myself to stay in abusive relationships and it indirectly led to me contracting HIV. In short, I cared too much for others, and much too little for myself. However, as an out and proud gay teacher in Secondary School and lecturer at university, I know that my ability to connect with people has given me the power to motivate and inspire many young people. I am very proud of this.

In recent years, I have embarked on a fantastic journey of self-exploration and have been able to address the fatalistic way of thinking that has derailed me in the past, every so often. As I write this, I am standing at the cusp of starting a new life in Melbourne, in Australia. I have never been happier.

So it all kind of worked out in the end. It might have taken me almost 46 years to get to this point in my life, but reconnecting with who I was as a teenager and a young man certainly helped me to heal the past. I wish I could actually go back in time and really say this to myself. But in lieu of time travel, I'm given a chance to say these words to other gay men who hopefully will find some reassurance.

Dear Paul,

Listen up. There is much I want you to know.....

I talk a lot to you in my head. It's funny and ironic because right now, I know you think that you don't have any power over people... I still sometimes trick myself into thinking like this as an adult, to this very day. The real truth is that you actually have GREAT power over MY adult life.

I am here for you NOW and I am holding you in my arms. Don't be afraid of me. I'm reaching deep inside myself to quell your fears, doubts and demons. I understand your passion, your resentment, your pride, your anger. You are not wrong in having these feelings. However, they are only a tiny spectrum of who you truly are... like tears in an ocean. You are a good kid, and I am blessed to have you.

I know you are hurting deeply right now. Growing up in suburban Surrey, where the normal middle-class life in England is a prize to be coveted, is difficult especially if you are slightly different. You try to fit, you try to please people and you hide your true self. By doing this, you are hurting even more. I understand what you are going through.

I admire you in so many ways. I miss your energy and sometimes wish that I had some of it back in my life right now. However, I plead with you to be kind to yourself. People may tell you that your sensitivity is a weakness; I am here to tell you that it will always be a strength. Please, please, please trust it, and trust yourself.

You will probably get angry with me when I tell you there is nothing wrong with you, Paul. This is because you feel threatened by my care and concern – you might even lash out at me in pride and in spite. Nonetheless, I will stand by you. You don't have to prove anything to me. Just be yourself. You are good enough. You don't have to try so hard. You have the strength and energy to make it through.

Right now you are trying so hard to be brave and strong by swimming through this stormy sea in which you find yourself. If you just keep your stroke, day by day, strong and steady, you will find that dry land is not too far off. Although you may not see it just yet, it's there. It's BIG, it's bold and it's a brave new world.

You certainly are not 'useless', even though this is repeated and repeated like a mantra by those who are meant to be your family of caregivers. When I look at you right now, I don't see a fat, tubby and ugly boy. Instead, you are bright, cute, friendly and very sweet. Your feelings of 'ugliness' have more to do with something else... feeling uneasy and unloveable because you think there is something unacceptable about a part of you. It's only a part Paul. Not a whole... and the irony is that this small part is perfectly acceptable.

And now for a note of caution...

Do NOT tease or make fun of Jonathan Mugle. I know that at school you and the other kids take even his name to be a mockery. Am I right to say that if you are a 'mugler' you are indeed 'bent' or 'queer'? Isn't that what you say in the school playground?

Jonathan is a very brave boy. He is strong and proud and alone and bold and fabulous. Everyone, including you, knows he is hiding a not so very well-kept secret. He actually has a boyfriend and is very happy in himself. So, don't punish him for being different and having the boldness to be happy with himself.

If you look inside yourself, you will see that bullying him is not just a smoke-screen for your own 'secret' but also because you are confused by the fact that he is comfortable with who he is. Don't do anything you will deeply regret later. If you lay a finger on him it's as good as hurting your own self. Remember where you come from and how much you hurt.

In a year from now, you will start life afresh as a young gay man in London. Yes, it will happen. You will cross paths with Jonathan Mugler again and instead of outing you as one of his schoolyard persecutors, he will reveal himself as one of your life's heroes. So, please be kind to him and see him for the brave and even exotic young man that he is. You will suffer very much later in your life if you don't listen to me now. Don't shame yourself Paul. Please don't.

School is tough and you too get your fair share from the bullies. But I tell you; you will triumph in the end. This is hard to believe now, but the very thing people are mistreating you for now, the very thing that you imagine right now will destroy your dreams, will actually, in the end, help you realize all your dreams beyond your wildest, wildest imagination.

Your kindness, your compassion and your originality all come from these experiences of feeling somehow different from the rest of the crowd. You will turn out to be a very clever man and you are and will be loved by some extraordinary friends. You will touch and inspire the lives of many of your students. In fact, they will call you 'Uncle P' because of all the love, care and nurture you will give to them.

As you grow older, you will learn that anger at injustice can be a great thing and it can help to instigate change in the world. It will help you find your voice. You will actively participate in many worthy and exciting events, wonderful marches and demonstrations. You will do this because you want to be a part of 'something'. It will prove to you that while the wheels of oppression turn for you, you can still show compassion and outrage at others caught up in the same machinery. However, remember that whilst you are taking a stand for others, YOU too are worth standing up for in this world.

You will meet many beautiful, creative, original and charismatic people along the way. But guess who really comes through for you most in your life? Your family! They will learn to accept you, love you, cherish you and applaud you. Your sister will become one of your best friends. Your mother will take her time to get her head around your sexuality, but she will do her best. Remember how it took you quite some time to be ok with being gay? Please be patient with her, it will take her some time because for her, it is also a journey towards acceptance.

Dad is going to be a revelation. I know you can't stand him now, but in a very unique way he will prove himself to be one of the best friends you will ever have. He will turn out to be one of your greatest supporters, who will say the most extraordinary things about you in your praise. He will even counsel Mum towards accepting you. I am telling you this now: you won't know about any of the things he'll do for you, until he is gone from this world. It is sad, but wonderful and true. So, please see him now as he is.

Please accept that for some people, especially those of an older generation, having a gay child is also a tough journey towards acceptance. Perhaps even a longer one than what it was for you. Once they understand that there is nothing 'wrong' with you, it will put them on a path where they too will have to stand in the face of a society that suggests otherwise. This will be an awakening for them and it won't be easy for them. It will take some time, but they will get there, and they will stand by you. They will even thank you in their own way for being a force for change in their lives.

I love you. Look forward to your life. It's gonna be an amazing ride.

Yours with love,

Paul

"Ordinary riches can be stolen, real riches cannot.
In your soul are infinitely precious things that
cannot be taken from you."

Oscar Wilde

Robert - 48

I was born in Trinidad, in the Caribbean, in 1964 to an Asian, Hindu father and Muslim mother who both converted to Catholicism after their marriage. We had a fairly middle-class upbringing even though we came from a relatively poor background. My dad was extremely ambitious and focused. He worked constantly and I seldom saw him, and when he was home, he barely interacted with me. I am the third child of four. My brother Trevor, is five years my senior and my sister Susan is three years older than I am. My baby sister, who is eleven years my junior, came much later and she has not played a major role in my life...

As the firstborn son, Trevor was my father's favourite child. He often took Trevor, on his own, to see my grandmother, who was matriarchal and quite formidable. My father also spoiled Susan terribly and showered her with many gifts, sparing no expense on her. Susan was a bit of a princess and seldom did any house chores, whereas my mother and I were like Cinderella: cooking, cleaning, laughing and talking.

My mother treated me very much like her husband and I heard many things a boy should never hear about his father, the reason being that my father had two other kids with a local woman and my mother did not know about this until after she married him. This caused her tremendous pain and they argued about it throughout their married life. My father was incapable of understanding that he did something wrong. He was the eldest and only son in his family; they treated him like a king, and he expected the same from my mother.

Since I was small, I have always been a people-pleaser, which counted in my favour because I was a nerdy and geeky child, and I struggled to make friends. I was painfully thin and rather unattractive compared to my muscular brother and beautiful sister, which did not help matters very much. I never felt loved and many Christmases I received hand-me-down bikes and Scalextric car racing sets that my brother didn't want any more. My parents saw nothing wrong with this. Until his death, a few months ago, I never heard the words "I love you" from my dad. I can probably count the number of hugs he gave me on half a hand. I hugged him once at the airport, which was terribly embarrassing for both of us and we never did it again.

Our neighbour's son sexually abused me when I was 5. We knew them well and I trusted him when he called me, and I was completely unaware of what was going on. However, I still have vivid memories of what happened and I remember the surroundings and all the smells... It took me several years of psychotherapy and self-improvement workshops to come to terms with it. This single event shaped my future and had an immense impact on my self-esteem and self-worth, which had an effect on many of the decisions I've made in my life.

When I was 16, my brother invited me to a Christian retreat with his girlfriend, and I became a reborn-Christian. I was so pleased that my brother took an interest in me (more than usual) and I happily tagged along. I definitely felt the presence of God during this experience. I tried to come out during the meetings, but was told that I was just confused and actually straight. They warned me not to mention it to anyone, because being gay would affect my future and how people 'viewed me'. Nonetheless, to this day, I still have not had a change of heart regarding my faith, even though I have difficulty reconciling my lifestyle with my beliefs.

In 1982, I started my studies in England. It was my first taste of freedom and liberation. I loved it and it felt like I was finally coming home. It was the time of the New Romantics, so I experimented with changing my hair colour, wearing alternative punk and rock clothing, and playing with a bit of makeup.

However, I never went to any wild parties, nor did I have any sex. In fact, I stayed a virgin throughout my university days and never told anyone that I was gay... I was too petrified of being rejected and judged. One Christmas (when I chose not to go home because I could not stand my parents' constant arguments), I stayed at the local Catholic chapel. I felt so low that I went looking for a gay bar in the east end that I saw advertised in a magazine. I never found it!!

I got involved with a Christian organisation. We went to church a lot and spent many hours doing bible study but it was difficult to connect with the guys I met there. After leaving university, I trained to become an actuary and I stayed on the straight and narrow by living with a Christian couple, which fed my need for Catholic restriction and control. However, I became increasingly aware of my attraction towards men... For instance, one day, a guy approached me in the showers at the public pools... Shortly afterwards, another man winked at me as I looked at him from the bus on my way home... It felt quite nice; however, I didn't dare to try anything. Instead, when anything like this happened, I quickly ran away.

I moved in with a guy whom I knew through the Christian couple I lived with. Daniel* was very attractive — your typical boy-next-door beauty. I became quite obsessed with him. We did many Christian activities together and were good friends. After living together for about a year, I decided to tell him that I liked him. Daniel did not take it very well. He started not to come home at all and when he did, it would be very late so that he didn't have to see me. It was horrible and my heart felt like it was breaking in two. I don't remember ever crying as much as I cried during that period. It made my 'coming out' a horrendous experience. Luckily, I had support and care from a very compassionate next-door neighbour. Though I wasn't suicidal, I wouldn't have survived without her. To this day, we are still friends.

Shortly after my path separated from Daniel's, I met Sarah*, an old acquaintance from the Christian organisation I used to be involved with. She was an attractive woman with a glamorous job in the music industry. She was obviously into me. I was attracted to her too, but in hindsight, I realise that I was on the rebound. We officially started dating about six months after meeting up again. To my disgrace, I remember two incidents that happened before I started going out with Sarah:

I sometimes stayed with a friend of my father, who was a high Anglican priest. He had a beautiful parish priest, who looked surprisingly similar to Daniel. The priest knew I was attracted to him. We kissed once. It made me feel so ashamed that I refused to see him again. He kept writing the most beautiful letters to me, begging me to keep contact with him. I never replied.

The second incident happened at a music event Sarah and I went to. A journalist made a pass at me and I responded. Sarah was in the room next door, and even though everything happened within seconds and she knew nothing about it, I felt terrible afterwards and decide to tell her that I was gay. She was quite good about it and asked me if I wanted to live 'that life' or be with her... I chose her, which set the wheels in motion for me living a straight life as a gay man...

Sarah and I got married in 1990. I was a virgin on our wedding day. My life was tumbling in a direction that was not of my own choosing. I was still the people-pleaser, doing what my friends, family and society expected from me. We never had great sex... Sarah's sex drive was a lot higher than mine was and I often felt pressured into doing it. I had never been with a man, so I didn't understand the concept of what that might be like, and neither did I ever think about it while I had sex with my wife. Sex with her happened fairly naturally.

My two beautiful children were born and Sarah became far more interested in them and their lives, while I was beginning to feel more and more side-lined. Even though we had great dinner parties and went on amazing trips and holidays, I never really felt complete. We were heavily involved in the church, but even there I was not connecting with people or making any real friends.

After 12 years of a very happy and stable marriage, I started to lose interest. With the onset of the Internet, I was spending more and more time on gay dating sites chatting to strangers. I once met a gay man who was also married. We kissed once, but the attraction waned quickly even though we had an amazing camaraderie... We are still friends today.

When I turned 40, I had my very first proper gay encounter. I met Charles* at the gym and we had been chatting for over eight months. He was "partnered" (though I thought he meant married to a girl). Charles was extremely attractive, very muscular, confident and funny. What attracted me to him was not his high-flying career but the fact that he was emigrating to Australia in a few months. For me, this meant a beginning and an end that posed no threat to my marriage, while I experimented with gay sex.

Charles asked me out for a drink one evening and I took the chance. We talked about the 'activities' in the gym's sauna and steam room. Though I turned a blind eye, I knew what was going on, because whenever I entered there would be a frantic kerfuffle of guys 'covering up'. Charles then invited me to go to a gay sauna with him. I realised I could go in one of two directions: take this opportunity and have my first gay experience with a wonderful and beautiful man, or let it pass me by. I said yes. It was the first time I actually made love to someone. It was amazing and we continued to have sex, almost daily, until he left for Australia.

When Charles left, I went into a downward spiral. It was the beginning of the end of my marriage. I did everything to fix things, from having 'Christian treatments' to psychotherapy and attending numerous self-help courses and workshops.

Though many of these helped me with integrity issues, healing my past and regaining self-worth, none of them changed my sexual orientation.

Approximately three years ago, Sarah said to me that she wanted me to be more committed and involved in our marriage. Our sex life had dwindled to virtually nothing for quite a while. I felt helpless and trapped. In the end, she asked me to leave and again I could choose only one of two directions. I decided to go. I moved out and even though my new home was relatively close to where Sarah and I lived, I felt alone and isolated. I was afraid to go out on the gay scene. When I did, once a guy showed interest in me, I would run away as soon as they came anywhere close.

Eventually I realised, through therapy, that my fear of trusting men and not allowing them to get close to me was all connected to the sexual abuse of my childhood. I have now accepted what happened and I don't allow the past to rule my future anymore. I have found a new freedom and have learned how to have a bit of fun and let myself go. I know I am making up for lost time.

I have a great relationship with my children and even though they are not living with me, I make every effort to spend as much time with them as possible. They are wonderful kids and our initial concern that our divorce would badly affect them was un-founded. My daughter did extremely well in the GCSEs and my son is an outstanding student.

I still care deeply for Sarah and we have managed to remain close friends after our divorce. In fact, she is one of my best friends. Luck-ily, she has an amazing family which grounds and supports her and the kids tremendously. In hindsight, I realise I should've been more honest with Sarah and let her in much sooner, however I was so terrified of rejection.

Being openly gay is a new chapter in my life and I am extremely hopeful of all the possibilities that lie ahead. I am happy that I'm finally living a life which isn't a half truth. It's been a tough journey, but I have accepted myself for who I truly am. I told my parents and as expected, they went completely crazy... Both my mother and father were very angry, but before his death, I sensed that my father had made peace with it.

I realise I can't live for people every second of my life. I've got to live for me as well. I can unequivocally say that the path I have chosen means that finally I am being who I should be. My mates joke about my clothes and muscled appearance, however, I don't mind. I finally feel alive and I don't intend to stop living till I am called by God.

I have a real heart for our community, but I do sense that something is missing or lost. I'm no expert and neither do I want to pass judgement on people that I love and care about. However, I struggle to understand why certain destructive behaviours are still considered the norm within the gay community, like substance abuse, alcoholism and binge drinking. I understand that the majority of us (even though some are still slow to admit it) are plagued with shame and fear... like me.

Perhaps it's time to reach out for an anchor, something positive and constructive, which could possibly enable a much-needed paradigm shift in the way our community perceives itself.

Dear Bobby,

I really wish I could talk to you now having learnt the things I have learnt.

First, let me tell you that you are perfectly fine.

I know the loneliness you felt, the lack of appreciation, the feeling that you were not good enough, not sufficient, and not loved in the same way as Susan and Trevor. I really wish I could hug you now and be there for you. I do understand why you started to disconnect from your emotions back then.

I understand how you realised that you 'don't get something for nothing' and that unless you cut the mustard, no one would notice you. I am so sorry that you never really had special friends or people that actually loved to be in your company. You had so much to give. You were loving, witty, funny, sweet and yet no one appeared to be bothered.

Worse still, when you tried to be authentic you were taught that it's dangerous and wrong to be so, and that it was best to keep it a secret.

I'm sorry that Mummy put you through so much unfairness by telling you stuff she really shouldn't have shared regarding your dad. You tried to be loving and caring, but it separated you from your father and men. It was unfair of her to treat you like you were her husband. This had a fundamental and detrimental effect on your life and was incredibly unfair.

I want you to know that you are a bright, witty and very loving boy, and certainly worth knowing. You are a real blessing to people and it was a shame that they never took the time to get to know you.

You are a great person and you will do great things. I wish people acknowledged this in you.

You are perfect and perfectly acceptable exactly as you are.

Love,

Rob

*"Be true to yourself
and you can't go wrong..."*
Tim

Tim - 51

My father was in the army in Singapore and when the time came for my family to return to Britain, he decided to stay behind. I was 6 or 7 years old. My dad disappeared from our lives for twenty years.

Back in Britain, we moved in with my grandparents, where we lived in a caravan. We were incredibly poor. The breakdown of her marriage was tough on my mother. Her way of making up for 'lost time' was to have many boyfriends and she got herself into quite a few scrapes. Fortunately, my grandparents were there for us and they loved us unconditionally.

I left school with no qualifications, and for a few years had a couple of dead-end jobs. When I was 17, a friend encouraged me to return to study but I clearly remember saying that I was too old but nonetheless went to a technical college, where I took eight 'O' Levels and two 'A' levels.

As a young adult, sex was not a pleasant experience for me. I fooled around with girls and had no problem talking to them and I was popular, I was 'the funny one', I made them laugh but sexually I did what I had to do. Occasionally I would get very drunk and have sex with guys – regretting it when the alcohol had worn off. The guilt, shame and disgust would then set in. Hating myself. I would be embarrassed to my core and the thought of anyone finding out was a great deal to bear.

Aged 22, I auditioned and interviewed at a number of colleges to study drama. I settled on going to a collage in Leicestershire and gained a BA (Hons) in Performing Arts. I wanted to get away from my family and experience living in a different part of the country. This was when I came into my own. The people I befriended during this formative and influential period are still close to me and will always be in my life. They are the ones who have seen me grow and once I came out, they accepted me as a gay man. Their support and acknowledgement of who I truly was helped immeasurably.

When I told my mother that I was gay (in my early twenties), she said to me: "Please don't tell me this. It makes me feel as though I have failed." That was a long time ago and since then she's become a great deal more accepting. She's been to stay with me and my boyfriend at our home a few times. I remember the first time she brought us both a cup of tea in our bedroom: she was shaking but managed to sit down and have a conversation with us both while we were still in bed. That small gesture meant a huge amount to me. She was trying and managing her prejudices, that meant a lot. My two older brothers and my sister are completely accepting of my homosexuality, it is not an issue for them. We have a very strong relationship, none of us is perfect but we support each other the best we can.

I am now a qualified therapist and have my own private practice in Soho and North London. I am in a great relationship and am very happy with my life at present. I still miss not having had a father. My dad is alive, but we've been apart for too many years. Us making up for lost time seems impossible.

When I see a film, or read a book about 'father/son' relationships, I get very emotional. Even when I watch the Simpsons on television, seeing Bart and Homer spending time together (and that's a pretty dysfunctional relationship), I feel I have missed out on the love of a father.

Unconditional love is what we all need and with that, life would be just that little bit easier.

Dear Tim,

I love you unconditionally
I love you and all that comes with that love
You are an individual, whatever you say or do is perfectly ok
I won't always agree with you but that's ok
I will support everything you do
You are funny
You are smart
You are loving
You will get things wrong
You will get things right
Be honest with yourself
Listen to others, but make your own decisions
You are exceptional
It will be rough at times but you will be ok

I love you.

Tim

*"Great spirits have always encountered violent opposition
from mediocre minds."*

Albert Einstein

Neil - 55

I was born in 1957 in a large market town on the coast of South Wales, surrounded by many coal mines and railways. It was an industrial base with car factories, breweries and steel works. It also had its own very famous rugby team. It was a society where men were men and those who weren't were looked down upon. Homophobia was rife and the norm in the community.

I was the second son of four siblings and we were brought up in a small guest house that my mother ran. My father was a public lighting engineer. Sadly, he was an alcoholic, so he wasn't around too much. I remember him, at that time of my life, as a man who was unapproachable. His sad addiction meant that he was selfish, at times stern, and he had little time for family.

One night, at the age of around 7, I got up from bed with a tummy ache. I went into our private family room where my mother was chatting to one of the more regular guests while busy doing the ironing. The guy lifted me onto his lap, cuddled me and rubbed my tummy affectionately. This was when I first felt an intimate connection with another man. I'm not sure whether it was prepubescent attraction on my part or just more about him having a very hairy chest: it was warm and fuzzy and I felt very comforted.

When I was 11, puberty arrived, and me and some friends at school started exploring each other's bodies. When they stopped, I wanted to carry on and realised that I was somehow 'different'. Shortly afterwards, I was fooling around with a mate in the woods: he dared me to the point that I was nearly naked. Then he abruptly ran off with my trousers. I was so humiliated when I noticed other kids from school laughing at me as I chased after him butt naked. The following year, I developed a crush on a boy in my class and scrawled his nickname all over my school books. It didn't feel wrong to me. I was just expressing myself. However, my classmates noticed this and I became the object of their ridicule, so I quickly changed the emphasis of my scribblings and vehemently denied that I was a 'queer'.

The following summer, before joining the army, my older brother started a gang. He was also exploring his sexuality but more vigorously than me with less to lose — the initiation ritual for gang members involved inappropriate contact with my brother. This provoked anger and gossip amongst boys from different schools. When I returned to school after the holidays, I bore the brunt of my brother's actions over that summer. I was tormented, shamed and bullied every day.

Meanwhile my brother wrote to me. His handwriting was almost illegible and I didn't realise that his letter contained some highly inappropriate content. Unfortunately, my mother discovered the letter and realised the nature of it. She wasted no time in referring the matter to my father who demanded an explanation. He bellowed at me, 'Are you fucking queer?' He told me that if I was, then I may as well move out. But I was only 13... how could I possibly survive...? So I was forced to deny all aspects of my sexual identity... and so I discovered a life of shame, hiding, secrets and lies.

At school, as word got around, I soon became known as the school 'poof', I was bullied every day for two years. Twice I got queer-bashed by a dozen or so (mainly unknown) kids in the centre of town. My only school friend ran off and left me to suffer the beating on my own. Why the hell did I deserve such a horrible fate? I discovered later in life that, unfortunately, this sort of thing happened to lots of people during this era.

Around the age of 14 I was working at my gran's market bakery stall and during my lunch break, 'youthfully frustrated' and in need of the toilet, I popped into the market lavatory. Whilst relieving my teenage frustrations, I was shocked to see a note on a piece of toilet paper being waved at me from under the adjacent cubicle wall. Nervously (but curiously) I read the note and was persuaded to meet up later in the day.

When I met the guy, we fooled around a little but nothing too serious happened. By now, I had learned to be strong and to do things on my terms. He told me that public toilets were the place where 'people like us meet'. He also told me where to find these places. He was older, about 35, and married with two kids. Prior to meeting this man, I did not know that there were other 'people like me' in any place, anywhere or that they even existed.

I had no one to talk to about my feelings, I couldn't talk to my parents, I had no real friends and spent most of my time in solitude. I became a loner. A few weeks after meeting the man in the toilet, quite by chance, while innocently in a park, I discovered another place where 'people like me' met. I was inquisitive... contact was made. Although I was excited and thrilled at the prospect during that long summer, every pleasurable encounter was with much older men. None of this felt 'wrong' because I finally found other men like me, that I could associate with. However, there was no friendship, in fact it always finished with 'I promise not to tell!' After all, I was also under-aged. A desperate loneliness and confusion filled my life. Much as I was relieved that there were other guys like me, I also had a compelling guilty feeling of shame about what we did in the park. And I remember thinking, "Is this the life I am destined to lead?"

I had to be vigilant all the time out of fear of homophobia, bigotry, lack of understanding and the small-town mentality of the self-righteous. As well as that aching feeling of guilt for being dishonest, a new fear of disgrace for improper behaviour emerged — being caught by the police. Even those secret meetings with the men I associated with were rubber-stamped with the parting promise of secrecy, and brought a feeling of disgust. This fuelled my feelings of shame and guilt for just being me. I just wanted to escape, I was depressed and at times, I felt suicidal.

Approaching my fifteenth birthday, I realised that I sneaked around town like a thief. Life became so dreadful. Everyone had deserted me and I had nobody to confide in. I was confused, alone and felt an outcast from society. I was overwhelmed and it all became too much. I left school. I also left home. In fact, I left the whole god-damn town and took a job twenty miles away, only to continue in secrecy what I had learnt. Shortly afterwards my parents split up.

Later, at 16, having started a college course, I returned to my gran's home for a weekend where my mother was staying.

During the weekend, someone who was previously very close (who will remain anonymous) attempted to blackmail me into having sex with him or else he would tell mother that I was 'a queer'. He succeeded with his blackmail attempt — simply because I couldn't deal with what I now understand to be the compounded shame. Prior to this, I was very close to this person and considered him a distant but dear friend. By doing this to me, he had betrayed me in the most terrible way.

This betrayal alongside my horrific early sexual experiences had a ripple effect through my life. Regretfully, I've betrayed many ex-partners and even lied to friends. Perhaps I'm a poor communicator? After writing this, the truth still no longer gets stuck in my throat and won't come out — it's out. I remember many occasions when I used to get emotional in inappropriate situations because I'd learned not to express my feelings. Over the recovery years I have realised that not being able to 'Just Be' I betrayed myself and others many times over, through a lack of trust in others and not knowing how to Love.

One of the most profound effects on my life was having to leave school before my fifteenth birthday. My education and development was massively affected. I often ask myself: why should learning have to be affected for some of us; people who just wish to advance their education and not expend their energies dealing with narrow-mindedness and mediocrity?

I blushed like a beetroot until I was 36 for little or no reason, and I lacked self confidence in many situations. I used to over-compensate by being a workaholic, being funny and telling stories, so that people didn't see my weaknesses. However, I used to go into hiding before people started digging deeper and discovered my sexual identity. I wasn't totally out until I was 42.

I'm sometimes sad at the lost opportunities, friendships, career stuff and all sorts, because of the fear that people would find out about my sexuality.

In the past I've had the need to always be in control and I'm the perfect planner — an endless list-writer, I've had problems finishing tasks, because I am scared of being judged on the end result. Perfectionism in a way used to be my prison, because I always have to do better. I've strived to manage my time and relationships - often with difficulty. When I've achieved, I've found acknowledging praise and thank-you's difficult.

When I was 20, I reminded my father of his threat when I was 13. He couldn't remember it but tried to explain his reaction. He accepted my sexuality and told me that he loved me. It meant the world to me but, unfortunately, he died quite young... It would've been great to have him around for a little bit longer, he turned out to be a very loving man with a fantastic sense of humour. Later in life I realised that I've inherited his 'addictive gene' and spent more than twenty-five years in a bubble before I started to break free from my own quick fix, addictive behaviours.

It turns out that my mother always loved me, but remained severely troubled with my sexuality. Her love for many years was conditional, not unconditional, as any son or daughter might hope for. Her refusal to accept who I was encouraged lies and dishonesty. Perhaps this is what inspired stubbornness in me, which led to us not speaking for almost twenty years. During this time she once wrote, "We all have our crosses to bear; your cross is to accept that we don't approve of the way you choose to live your life." Although I hated those words at the time, looking back similar attitudes have certainly left their marks and challenged my life in many ways. It would have been great to experience a positive role model. Eventually, my mother finally apologised to me and welcomed my partner into her home. It was a massive breakthrough and paved the way to rebuilding bridges that I thought burned and destroyed. I am now actively working towards healing our relationship: my benchmark is to be comfortable to call her "Mum". This process has made me realise that I made a subconscious decision at the age of 13 to call her "Mother"; it was an emotionless label and about biological function.

I'm in the second decade of recovery from life's challenges and addiction, thankfully rarely approaching crisis — confident to deal with and share my feelings. That baseline feeling of 'you're not good enough!' and struggling to be who I am, to place myself above the parapet wall and stand up for what I believe in has dissipated. I'm nearing the end of dealing with the affects that bullying and homophobia have had on my life; the last bastions of perfectionism and the deep-seated sense of low self-esteem. The recovery from the debt of endless feel-good quick fixes, poor communication and over-compensating generosity will be an on-going journey well into my retirement. Still, I feel I have achieved so much in the past thirteen years with much work on my personal development to reach a safe and comfortable place of self-acceptance. Because of the challenges I've dealt with, I know that I am a much stronger, tenacious, reliable, and more thoughtful person. I've learned to be less generous and more giving. I've learned to worry less and trust more.

Over the intervening years I have experienced, witnessed and heard of much homophobia. Attitudes in society have taken decades to change. Even now — forty-five years on from the repeal of anti-gay laws, there's still a considerable way to go to change the prejudice in many parts of society.

I am happy to say that just at the right time in my life I have connected with a lovely, special man on a level which I've never experienced with anyone else. We have been together for more than four years. He's loving, empathetic, intelligent, funny, witty and gorgeous. He supports me, and most of all he sorts my head out. He is the light of my life.

This year we were planning a civil partnership but we've decided to wait and go the whole hog: to wait and get married when the law is changed.

All I ever wanted and all I ever needed in my life is here, in my life and in my heart now. Now is about just Being. Be in the present and embrace life.

My Dearest Neil,

I'm so sorry that you feel so alone, abandoned and confused. All of this happening during your formative years only makes matters worse. All you need is support, guidance, love and acceptance. You have been treated appallingly by everyone close to you and everyone around you. The community that you lived in is homophobic and nothing less than hostile and you have little means of escape at this time.

Please be assured that, sometimes in life, one has to make sacrifices and this demonstrates a great maturity. The pain of your sacrifices will fade away, even if it doesn't feel like that for you now. It's best not to reveal your sexuality, because the people around you are very narrow-minded. So, for the time being, be careful about displaying your emotions. Limit your explorations to the same as the boys around you, stop when they stop and don't get sucked into clandestine meetings later in your teens.

Stay focused in school, you are doing well so continue with your education. Explore university perhaps, because this will facilitate more opportunities and competencies and bring more choices into your life. You will be able to celebrate, with confidence, your difference and to learn to love who you will become. There will be plenty of time later in your life for exploration and Love.

There are many people like you, and as you get older, you will settle in one of the greatest, most cosmopolitan cities in the world. You will meet many, many lovely people like yourself. You will have many great friends who will love you for who you are, not for who they think you should be. In fact, they will treat you as their family even when your own family is not supportive. You will find much happiness and be with the man of your dreams. So take heart!

Be aware and try to respect that different things come to different people at different times. People struggle with fundamental principles but while they do, you must know that we are all equal, we should not be judgmental. Celebrating and embracing our differences is what makes life interesting and wholly enriching.

Sadly, people say and do wicked things, often without thinking through the consequences. It's often the case that people's experiences later in life may give an opportunity to reflect and review what they have done to others.

Dad will eventually grow to love you, sooner than you think, and you will be close with each other. He will respect who you are, and equally love who you are with. He will love your friends and he will be loved by them. He will be happy to see what you have done with your life and he will be very proud of you.

Know that when you grow up, you will have a greater understanding of life's complexities. You will be able to persuade Mum to accept and love you for who you are. Yes, this takes time and you will need to respect other people's learning journeys too.

Be assured that you are kind, creative, generous and giving. You are a bright, very lovely young man. You have a wonderful sense of humour and a tenacious character. Do not feel ashamed of who you are, and you will survive this.

Be true to yourself within yourself – throw away all self-doubt, because your time will come, okay? You will be accepted and you are destined to marry a man.

Take care of yourself.

With much love,

Neil

SHAME

Darren Brady

When I did a slow dance with my boyfriend in front of my family.
When a football heads in my direction in a park
and I go to kick it back.
When my uncle asks if I have a partner.
When I think of my failed relationships.
When I am in a room with lots of gay men.
When I watch TV with my mum and there is a gay kiss.
When I see two men holding hands in the street.
When I am in a room full of straight men.
When I am alone with a straight man.
When I check in with a boyfriend at a hotel.
When another gay man looks at me on the tube, bus or street.
When I talk to a young child on the street.
When I pass by a group of teenagers.
When pushing a trolley round a supermarket with a boyfriend.

CHAPTER THREE

STRIVING TO SURVIVE

Our lives consist of an amazingly rich and intricate tapestry of circumstances; a complex mix of distinctive 'ingredients' and experiences that shape us and tell the world who we are.

In some instances, we have a choice in the matter, but with others, we don't get to decide — like whether we are male or female, have blue or brown eyes, where we were born and the families we inherit. However, we do have some power over the music we listen to, how affluent we are, and the rules and values we choose to obey, but we do not have to be a slave to them.

One of the things we don't get to choose is our sexuality. Human sexuality is not determined, for example, by where we live, how we grow up or the type of friends we hang out with. And yet it lays the foundation of the enduring emotional, romantic, and sexual attractions we feel towards men, women, or both sexes. It also influences non-sexual physical affection between partners, shared goals and values, mutual support, and on-going commitment which are essential parts of our personal identity. In short, our sexuality touches the core of our existence.

In *Oddly Out Of Place,* we explored how knowing that we are different from a very early age had an impact on our perception of ourselves and our place in the world. We saw how being at odds with our sexuality can lead to the cultivation of limiting beliefs. Along with this, as part of our deep-rooted fear of being viewed as the 'different one', gay men also develop survival strategies to instinctively protect ourselves or cover up what we are made to feel ashamed of.

We are no strangers when it comes to striving to survive. In this chapter, we continue to hear how gay men learn, from a very early age, to adapt to an environment that prevents us from expressing a fundamental part of our identity. We see how we develop strategies to help us survive. These survival strategies can either be a curse or a blessing.

As gay men, our survival instincts already kicked in during those early days when we first felt oddly out of place, and they continue to carry us into our adult lives on an unconscious level. Striving to survive is a response to a perceived or actual threat we experienced at some stage in our gay lives. It may be that we had to survive the emotional withdrawal of our parents and family, in response to our sexuality. Perhaps we needed to survive bullying or taunts from our classmates and peers, or the deep shame of feeling attracted to another boy in our classroom.

In order to survive, we developed behaviours that helped us get by. We become the funny ones, the inconspicuous ones, the charming and intelligent ones, or any number of other ways to distract attention from the thing we are ashamed of. In fact, the pages of this book are filled with numerous stories that recount these survival strategies. Whatever the circumstances, we learnt to respond, and we sought to survive.

Once we reach adulthood, our survival mechanisms are so habitual that we don't recognise them as such. They become so embedded in our being that we mistake them as characteristics of who we truly are. Unlike our limiting beliefs, our survival mechanisms often enable us to become highly successful. They may even propel us to exceptional heights or protect us from danger. We may be the wittiest of friends or the most charming of house guests. We may have channelled them to help us become famously expressive and creative or they form a part of our sensitive intuitive skills that enable us to support those around us. This is the blessing.

The curse of these survival strategies, on the other hand, is when they don't serve us anymore and we allow them to become our default setting, even in situations where we don't need them. As we get older, our survival mechanisms often backfire and no longer produce the same results they used to. Instead, they give us a sense of exhausting and continual struggle. They are no longer an asset, but have become part of a destructive and negative behaviour pattern and an avoidance mechanism.

Rather than surviving victoriously, we end up sinking miserably. It is a confusing state of affairs. We often don't link the behaviours that helped us through difficult times as being the very same behaviours that, as adults, are holding us back. We start to blame external factors for the state of our lives, rather than our limiting internal dialogue and behaviour. Our failure becomes the fault of our partners, our workload, family, society, money... the list goes on.

The chapter *Striving To Survive* illustrates how many gay men struggle between limiting beliefs, survival mechanisms and who they truly are. Without examining and challenging our thoughts and actions, these behaviours can end up dominating and suffocating our lives. We may become workaholics, addicted or reliant on substances such as alcohol or drugs; we may withdraw into debilitating depression or try to shop ourselves into happiness by buying the latest and greatest cars, houses and clothes.

Recent statistics from the UK charity Stonewall sadly indicate that gay men suffer disproportionately from all of these attempts to survive our lives. Once we fully understand the impact of hiding our sexuality and avoiding the pain of invalidation with self-defeating behaviours and redundant survival mechanisms, the real journey towards our true selves starts, and we can begin to undo the damage that has been done. We retrace the steps of our childhood, revisit the painful memories, and very importantly, we identify the decisions that we made at these critical times. At first these decisions protected us and for a short while helped us to survive, but ultimately they do not serve us moving forward.

As we piece together this map of limiting beliefs and survival strategies that we have constructed, and once we understand how they manifest in our lives, we can challenge their relevance and question their ability to sustain us in a place of happiness and fulfilment.

Striving to survive can be a stepping stone to a life which, with time and inquiry, can blossom from surviving into thriving.

Sadly some gave up.

Some give up.

We honour those who no longer strive and therefore do not survive.

"Toto, I have a feeling we're not in Kansas anymore."

Dorothy — The Wizard of Oz

David - 48

I grew up in a small town called Nelson, which is between Manchester and the Yorkshire Dales, in the UK. Nelson developed as a textile-manufacturing town during the Industrial Revolution in the mid-18th century. In the 1960s, most of the cotton mills closed down and the place went downhill fast. It became ridden with poverty, crime and hopelessness.

My father was a weaver, a magistrate and a union leader and my mother worked part-time as a secretary for solicitors and a Muslim organisation. Both my parents were British and Christian, but they came from completely different backgrounds. My father was from a poor working-class family. My mother came from a wealthy colonial family, who had lived in Arabia. They met in Austria, while my father was in the army and my mother was touring Europe.

Their contrasting backgrounds meant that I struggled to find my own identity. I felt out of place in Nelson and dreamed of the life my mother's family had before the war... travelling and living in exotic places, owning expensive cars and nice houses. None-theless, I still had a good relationship with my parents, but they always expected me to be strong and 'grown up'. This put me under a lot of pressure and made it hard for me to be honest about my feelings and ask for help.

School was horrible and rough. Most of my classmates and even some of the teachers had a sense of hopelessness. It was uncool to be clever and nobody had any ambitions or saw a better future for themselves.

At the age of 13, I knew that I was gay. Nevertheless, since my friends, father and society loathed gays more than anything else, I was terrified that being gay meant that I would be hated too. Oddly, I also feared and detested gay people, even though I'd never met any. This was because the only gays on television or in films were portrayed as sad, pitiful, predatory or laughable carica-tures. I couldn't identify with these characters. I felt very lonely and comforted myself by thinking: 'If I'm going to live a lonely life, at least I want to have money and travel the world.'

By the time I turned 16, there was nobody I could open up to and share my feelings with. This was the worst time in my life. However, when I reconnected with friends from school as an adult, I learned that I was not the only one who experienced those negative feelings... If I'd known this back then, things could've been different and I might have been able to talk to someone about how I felt.

Things changed for the better once I left school, even though I was still too afraid to come out. I convinced everyone that I was straight. I had good friends and a girlfriend... I told myself that I was bisexual and entertained fantasies about men but never acted on them. I had sex with women a few times but I didn't enjoy it. Something about it felt wrong... I was playing a character, trying to work out what people wanted me to be and then act accordingly.

Coming out took some time, but I have happy memories about it.

In 1984, I spent the summer working in the US. I was 20. During this time, I briefly met a gay couple. They were the first openly gay people I had ever met and I was surprised at how pleasant and 'normal' they were... For the first time, I considered the idea of coming out.

The next summer I worked in Kansas City. I spent the whole summer thinking about coming out... I was far away from home, so doing it would be 'safe' because none of my friends or family would ever know... Finally, I decided to go to a gay cruising area to pick someone up. This was more about meeting other gay people, than about having sex... I was so afraid, mostly because I still didn't trust gays. However, I met several great guys. One man in particular was really supportive and encouraging. It ·· as a very positive experience.

rned to university, I decided to come out to all my
family. By the end of 1985, I had told everyone I
credibly empowering. I enjoyed feeling brave and
proud.' Of course, there were some problems.

My family was fine, except for my father who said some horrible things, before he threw me out of house. Many of my friends also secretly freaked out, and avoided me once we left university.

After graduating, I moved to London and started work at an international bank. Within months, I had gay friends and lovers. I was travelling all over the world, and I bought a house and two cars. Life was good. At work no one knew I was gay, and I was happy to make this compromise because I saw how a senior colleague was victimised after rumours went around that he might be gay.

Over the years, I steadily came out at work and the more I stood up for myself, the more people accepted and embraced it. The same was true in the rest of my life and even my father eventually accepted my sexuality. I have seen how attitudes towards gay men have changed.

However, it's a pity that mainstream media still portray gays as harmless, sexless, camp, non-threatening and shallow. In my own life, I have rebelled against these one-dimensional stereotypes, because there is so much more to being a gay man.

Looking back, I've also realised a few hard truths: I explored every possible fetish, screwed around and travelled to sex parties around the world... It was fun, but maybe I chose sex, rather than relationships. There were plenty of drugs too and much as I never allowed them to control my life, they were still very destructive.

I often chose adventure, rather than stability. This includes suddenly moving abroad, because I was bored with my life in the UK. Being so inconsistent has undermined many wonderful relationships and friendships.

Finally, the values instilled in me as a child have made it difficult for me to be vulnerable and to really trust friends and lovers with my true feelings. I have paid the price for this, because people think either you don't need their help, or it drives them away because you're too strong and detached.

Dear David,

I know life is tough at the moment, and you feel totally alone and isolated. I understand. Your home town really is a dump, and the place is only going to get worse. But that's not the real issue, is it? It's all about friends... don't worry - your friends are having a pretty hard time too.

There's something you need to know.

The camp queens on television and the way your friends hate them isn't the truth. You don't have to be afraid of gay people or being gay. There are a lot of good gay people out there. More importantly, the people that scream hate at gays are the minority... and quite a few of them are just trying to hide their own sexuality!

Don't be afraid about being short or skinny, posh or common, shy or outgoing.

Don't be afraid to be yourself.

Take your time. You can take a lifetime to work out who you are, but don't be afraid to try.

You see, being honest about yourself isn't easy. You have to be honest in your own head, then be honest with the people around you. Only then will people know the real you. Some won't like that, but many will – and they will like the real you. Believe me!

Here's the strangest thing: when you stand up for who you are, even in a small way, you make small changes to the world around you. You change people's minds. You make others respect what you stand for. You give others courage to stand up for themselves. Ultimately, you make others respect you.

Life isn't about the car, the house or the job. Ambition is good but it's not everything. After all, someone will always have something better than you... Instead, life is about honesty: being happy and sad, brave and sensitive, supportive and vulnerable, wise and unsure.

Life is about discovering the real you. The things you love to do. The people you love and who love you (I'm talking friends, family and lovers). There is a wonderful world out there, and a place in it for you. You don't even know the half of it! You can be butch and camp, all at the same time. You can break those stereotypes, and enjoy playing with them too. You'll be totally one of the girls, and so much one of the guys.

But more than anything else, you will find people who love the real you. And some of them are already around you.

Be brave — it'll be worth it!

Love,

David

"...the only people for me are the mad ones,
the ones who are mad to live, mad to talk,
mad to be saved, desirous of everything at the same time,
the ones who never yawn
or say a commonplace thing, but burn, burn,
burn like fabulous yellow Roman candles
exploding like spiders across the stars."
Jack Kerouac

Giampiero - 36

I am originally from Italy, where I grew up in a large Catholic family. My biggest challenges as a child were coping with my older sister's mental illness. I was only 7 when she had her first schizophrenic episode. I quickly learnt that in our small community, mental illness was frowned upon and that there was very little professional help for people like my sister or my family.

My parents worked all day, and they left me and the other children alone at home to take care of my sister. I believed that her pain, suffering and well-being were my responsibility. I became her parent and felt that no-one was taking care of me. Her illness left my entire family with a feeling of emotional impotence and it filled me with a lot of bottled-up anger and frustration.

Because my parents had such a hard time coping, I decided from a very early age that, in order to please them, I would be a 'very good boy'. I stopped paying attention to my own needs. I did not want to be any trouble and stopped voicing my own desires. At school, the other kids started bullying me, because I did not stand up for myself. This made me feel even more like an outsider. I was unworthy and not good enough. I felt lost.

I never liked labelling people and always thought that when you fall in love, you do so with whomever you choose, man or woman. However, when I first started feeling attracted towards guys, I had no one to talk to, because I was so overwhelmed by the shame of living in a society filled with prejudice. I was confused and scared.

As I grew older, I struggled to build intimate relationships with both women and men, because I had no connection with my true self. I couldn't take responsibility for my feelings and had great difficulty expressing my emotions. At times, I would get overwhelmed by anger and fear, and react by looking for a quick fix by pursuing some sexual fantasy, just to stop feeling so anxious and overwhelmed... it was self-defeating behaviour that didn't serve me well at all.

I've since moved to London where I am now embracing all the opportunities to build a career in the travel industry and as a result I have travelled to many wonderful places. I'm also following my passions for the theatre, music and arts, and I'm actually going to a drama school. In the past, I wouldn't have done any of these things, because I had no self-worth. Now, when I engage with something that I love with all my heart, I remind myself of how important my own needs are.

Learning to put myself first has helped me to find the support I need to help my family to take care of my sister. It saddens me that, to this day, my sister still refuses to get counselling. She remains very ill. However, I am not running away from these problems anymore. I can see the value of all the beautiful people in my life and what they have taught me. I have been able to build strong friendships with wonderful people who allow me to share my life with them. This makes me very proud.

I'm at a place in my life now where I am slowly becoming the person that I want to be, even if it's someone completely different from what other people expect me to be... I am more in touch with my emotions and I express them better. I believe that my real needs are to be loved and accepted, and to take care of myself and the people around me... this is how I will become an even better version of the great person I already am.

Three years ago, I decided to tell one of my sisters that I am sexually attracted to men. She is the only member of my family who knows. I am currently dating a guy and much as I am on a path of discovering my true authentic self, I sometimes still struggle with feelings of inadequacy. However, I am aware that overcoming those feelings of unworthiness and to stop being afraid of getting what I really want and need in life is key to finding lasting happiness.

Dear Giampiero,

You are 16 now and I want to give you these words of support:

I know you are fighting against many difficulties in your life and you often feel that you are drowning. Sometimes you think you've lost everything and you look for a way to end it all.

All your life so far, you have searched for someone to listen to you and to help you when you were a victim of abuse. At home, you feel impotent and frustrated as you watch your schizophrenic sister's pain. You feel her agony and you suffer with her. Know this: the rest of your family feels the same. Sadly, sometimes things are just too overwhelming for people to deal with. Accept this reality: you are not responsible for curing your sister's mental health problems. You are only a child and just one person.

You feel a lot of anger, because you are being bullied at school. Don't blame others for your anger because, one day, you will end up blaming yourself. When you feel awkward and like an outsider, and you don't find a role model to look up to, remember there are many people going through the same things.

Love does not know gender. You can love whomever you want to: a man or a woman. Just follow your heart. Don't be scared when you feel you're not part of the crowd. It is challenging, but I am sure you will find the strength to express your unique and amazing self. You don't have to be a victim.

Although you don't have a parent who hears your voice now, later in life you will find the parent inside yourself, who will show you how to heal the wounds of the past. You will find the courage to get through the worst moments of feeling lonely. You will eventually start to manage your anger and stop hiding your true self and real needs. Once you know how to forgive, life will be less painful and you will learn to trust yourself. This is part of your amazing journey.

There will also be 'angels' like your friends, family and counsellors, who will help you realise that you are perfect, even with your imperfections. You will be overwhelmed by so much love from the people around you. You will learn how to use your strong emotions in a creative way and you'll see how those feelings will turn out to be your best friend.

Your passion for theatre will give you an outlet where you can use all your life experiences to express all your pain and joy. This will give you so much more confidence.

When you have doubts and the people around tell you that you can't follow your passions, and that you can't sing, hold on to your dream and listen to your heart. You will find the power inside your soul to pursue your dream. You will prove all of them wrong. Even the demonic voice of your paranoia and insecurities in your own head will go silent and will stop controlling you.

Reach high. Failing does not mean that you are not good enough. Be a dreamer! No one can take away the light that I can see inside you.

You have so much to give. You are brave, loving and caring. You will have so much joy that will fulfil your life. Keep your eyes on the big picture and remember that we are all little amazing elements, which are part of a much bigger universe.

You may not know your own strength now, but you will surprise yourself. You will eventually stand up for yourself again. Although you are in darkness now and your free spirit is hiding deep inside, the beautiful light inside you will shine through and your soul will show you the way towards life. Just listen carefully to him.

Be strong and remember that you are not alone.

Take time to find your way.
Learn to express your emotions.
I will help you to believe in yourself.
You will go on a spiritual journey
and one day you will know,
no matter what happens,
everything will be alright.

Fight for your beliefs
and you will find your true self,
happiness and contentment.
Follow your passions.
Love your mistakes.
These things are all a part
of who you are today:
An adult who takes responsibility,
who stands up for himself
and someone who has grown
to become a brave
and compassionate man.
Love your friends.
They will help you to live authentically
and to make intimate connections,
so you won't feel disconnected anymore.

Love whoever you are
and whomever you fall in love with.
Love without regrets
because life is the best thing you have
and it's too short to run away.
Show your whole shining self
because I am proud of who you are.

Love,

Giampiero

"Victor qui laborat - He who works, conquers."
Anonymous

John - 58

I come from a long line of working-class Lancastrian slaters (roof-tilers) and prostitutes. My great-great-grandmother took to the streets as the only way to keep her own five illegitimate children, and two of her sister's, in a mill cottage during the Cotton Famine of the 1860s, when two-thirds of the county was on parish relief.

I was born in the shadow of great events: the Queen's coronation and the conquest of Mount Everest both happened the week I was born, so it was relatively easy to slip unnoticed into the world. A much-longed-for only child, I grew up in Manchester as a happy, precocious, outgoing and bright kid before winning a scholarship at 11 for a 'free place' at a tough, rugby-playing traditional boarding school, where I simply didn't fit in.

I coped with the bullying by becoming invisible, deliberately underachieving in class to avoid standing out from the crowd, scoring beneath my potential during exams, and living a private fantasy life in my head. I felt that my fond but ambitious parents loved me a little less as a result of that, and blamed me for not being less shy.

I am not now religious, but I was baptised into the Church of England and enjoyed Sunday School and nativity plays as a small boy — although as a shepherd boy wearing a smock my mother had made from the dining room curtains, I felt humiliated at being told I couldn't use the boys' toilets in church because I was wearing a dress!

At 14 I declined confirmation, perhaps as a first rebellious act of 'not belonging'. However, I also did it partially to avoid staying after school for confirmation class. This reflected my shyness and attitude to groups for many years. University — where the atmosphere was more liberal — was a much better environment for me, although still adopting my parents' political views made it difficult for me to gravitate towards the 'gay lib' societies. I remained closeted until well after graduation, going through a confused period of going out with girls, even though I knew my true affections were for men.

After a first job in which the bullying wasn't much less than at school, and an insane three years in which I was a Conservative local councillor in Southampton (actually encouraged into it by a guy who'd answered my lonely hearts ad in Gay News), I moved to London aged 26 to live with a partner. There I found more acceptance, openness and opportunities, gaining confidence year-on-year, both professionally and as a gay man. I was 33 before I realised I didn't have to follow the path chosen for me by my parents, and that I was free to make my own way. Coming out wasn't painful, although my father ignored the statement and, until his death, told people that I had 'never met the right girl'.

Aged 36, I lost everything in the same two weeks: a creative job in a top architectural practice which went out of business, my boyfriend of 12 years, and my home. Throwing all the cards up in the air turned out to be a massive benefit, as I found new directions as a self-employed design consultant and worked directly for several of my previous clients at the architectural firm. Specialising in investment banks, my work took me around the world, living for a year in New York, and also working in Singapore and Moscow. I joined the London Gay Men's Chorus, found friends there, and have sung at the Royal Festival Hall, Carnegie Hall, and Sydney Opera House.

The night I sang at Carnegie Hall, on a stage across which my every musical hero from Yehudi Menuhin to Judy Garland had walked, I shed tears of regret that my parents died before I could share such happiness with them.

New York was a springboard to business success, too, and twelve years later I was able to give up full-time work. I now work as a theatre critic, live in a lovely riverside apartment, travel extensively for pleasure rather than for work, find time for charity projects and leisure activities, and feel that I have a good life.

My early experiences of feeling isolated made me independent and in a way strong-minded, but I also protected myself with a cynical attitude to other people and a readiness to criticise which may have put some off and meant I never enjoyed much in the way of optimism or hope, and treated even my long-term partners as accessories, rather than equals. Life is fine now, but I wish I'd been more open to other people along the way and shared more enjoyment of the journey.

Dear John,

The values you are being shown by your school, teachers, prefects and other boys will not translate into the wider society you will inhabit as an adult.

There are more devices, more ways and more opportunities to integrate into a community, than the one presented to you now. You will find the means to grow and to express yourself and your identity. You will also find outlets for the talents you are suppressing now, in order not to stand out and to cope with school.

You will be popular, if that's what you want. And you will find someone that 'gets' you and loves you because of that understanding.

There is no shame in feeling how you do, or in taking time to reach your potential. That's what potential is — something that's about to happen.

Feel its power with you and look ahead. You will have a good life.

Love,

John

"... because life is too short..."

Darren

Darren- 47

I felt it most as I found myself wandering around parks and streets... anywhere really... especially where crowds of people would meet and congregate. It was particularly bad on lovely hot sunny days, when spirits were high and people were happy. I just felt so separate from them; so apart and so lonely.

I would retire to the safety of my home and often stay there for a long time, hiding away from everything that I did not feel part of. I kept wondering: How can I engage? What can I do to feel connected with life again? During these periods of 'observing life', I felt an exhausting and lethargic malaise, which I only now reluctantly recognise as depression.

Something had to be done. So, I took myself off to a psycho-therapist. One of the first questions she asked me was: 'Do you remember when you first started feeling this sense of separation?' I pondered. Then the dreadful answer came to me: when I was 13, gay, and no longer part of the gangs and groups of kids playing happily in the streets, fields and play-grounds where I lived.

Surely, 30 years later I had processed and sorted out that painful period of my life?

Apparently not.

My memories of my early childhood years are blissful: a doting mother, loyal brother and dutiful father who created a secure, warm and stimulating home. All the photos of me as a baby till the age of 6 show a child full of wonder and joy. Then, suddenly, when I was 7, my father had a brain haemorrhage on Boxing Day and he died. Life changed dramatically.

The years following were marked by loss and isolation. Gradually, I felt the protection and closeness of my brother wither. I felt my mother withdraw into the loss of her beloved husband, and I started to clip my free and expressive wings as my behaviour ceased being amusing and became a cause for concern and scorn. My uncle once used the word 'poof' to describe me in front of the family, and I remember how much pain this caused me. I was under attack and the joy within me evaporated.

At school, I found my escape — drama. I was encouraged and allowed to be expressive. I was applauded and nurtured. I sought and found care, admiration and attention through performance and my drama teacher became my surrogate mother. After a couple of years in the wilderness of not fitting in, crying and being taunted by my brother, I found my tribe — a youth drama group. Suddenly I belonged to a group of creative misfits.

In my desperate struggle to belong, I found a place where I could thrive. I threw myself into this world with all my energy and commitment. I became a minor amateur dramatic celebrity! Within this bubble, I found expression but outside, in the wider world, I was at odds with a world that just did not speak to me.

I first went to a gay bar and had sex with a man when I was 17. However, it was only at the age of 21 that I first had a meaningful conversation with anyone about my sexuality. Twenty-one formative years with no communication or input about a fundamental part of myself had inflicted considerable damage and deep seated shame.

The feeling I experience in these moments can be sharp, stabbing and short lived. These are moments so fleeting, yet common, that I sometimes do not even recognise that they are there.

But they ARE there.

I ignore them, deny them and distract myself from them.

But they are there.

They ring my inside, they prod at a sore so deep and so wounded. I appear serene, beyond hurt and any pain.

But inside I twist and turn, desperately looking to escape from this shame — this feeling that I am wrong. Fundamentally wrong. And then in the next moment, I move on, I smile, I turn away, I get on with my life as if nothing happened; as if nothing lurks within me waiting to be exposed once more.

For most of my adult life, I have skilfully masked, avoided or distracted myself from a fundamental and painful sense of not belonging. So skilful that even I did not recognize my behaviour as such. I kept myself busy with having a 'fun time', moving house, travelling the world, being creative and skipping from one relationship to another.

This all was driven, in part, by a desire to get away from a sense of isolation. I was merely surviving life. A life that was turning itself into distinct and unhelpful (often destructive) patterns of behaviour that I could no longer ignore or blame others for.

In around 2004, I paused.

I started stopping.

I remember writing angrily in my journal at the time 'life just seems to be about taking things away and stopping. What new things will I bring into this life?'

I started meditating, reading self-help books. I sold the thriving business I had created thirteen years earlier. I bought a dog. I travelled to the East and studied Reiki. I retrained as a Life Coach. I stopped drinking alcohol and gradually, over time, even the disco dancing dwindled. I started to listen to myself and others in a way I had never done before.

As I withdrew the strategies for avoiding feeling alone, I started to feel really alone. Even more so when I was not in a relationship and so I found myself going deeper, looking inwards to reveal what lay at the heart of this distressing state. With the help of a therapist, I started to join the dots. Slowly everything started making sense and a new experience of life started to emerge.

I'm very much still within this new reality. Working with gay men, co-founding The Quest and embracing a curiosity for my life is revealing wonderful new possibilities every day. It gives me a sense of peace and belonging that I only remember being part of my life in my very early childhood.

Dear Darren,

Firstly, let me tell you that you are safe. You can look after yourself and there are people who love you who will also watch out for you. You will attack life with such spirit and engagement and life will reward you in return. You can trust your inner voice. Listen to what you tell yourself because those are the wisest words you will hear. Listen carefully and be advised even when the words are scary or strange or different from what others tell you.

You are loved and protected. You will be able to move ahead without having to fight all the way. Be soft. Allow yourself to feel your emotions and let your feelings surface. Say what you feel and all will be fine.

You are a sensitive soul and you think you have to be hard and strong but you can allow your softness to hold you, to take care of you and to guide you what to do. Sometimes your sensitivity will move you away from people, sometimes it will bring you closer. However, it will always have your care and happiness in mind and it will keep you safe.

You will get tempted to betray yourself. You will be tempted to let go of what you know is right for you. These are the moments where your strength comes in. Protect your sensitive soul.

You will do extraordinary things and you will have so much fun. You will always find a way through and you will always be creative. Keep connected to your creativity. Let it guide you. Let it flourish. Surround yourself with creative richness. Find those who share your energy and enthusiasm and trust. When in doubt return to your inner voice. If you get lost, return to this quiet place.

Everything you imagine is possible. Stay true. Stay trusting. Stay gentle.

Your family is not your enemy.
Others are not your rivals.
There is no battle.
There is no struggle.
You are welcome.
You are wanted.
You are fine.
You are wonderful.

You are a sensitive soul that loves and is greatly loved.

Your sensitive soul is the strength. It will protect you. It is your sensitive soul that will guide you, not the brute.

Be gentle, love, be held.

Love,

Darren

*"I love the courage I have been given to love and be open,
I love and live for the tingle down my neck,
and tears in my eyes,
the humour in my mind and heart,
and the stillness of my soul."*

Neil

Neil - 45

I read somewhere that clemency is the path to peace. As I'm working towards reaching a place of forgiveness, in some instances, I'm reliving my childhood. I'm not entirely sure who I'm supposed to be forgiving: myself, my parents, the guys who took advantage of me when I was looking for love as a young boy, or the mentor who raped and shamed me. I do my best to 'love' and 'admire' these people for what they've achieved in their lives. I also accept that my parents have done the best they could. Yet, I still keep my distance from all of them, because I feel they've taken something away from me.

My early childhood experiences have been the foundation on which I tried to build my adult relationships. I've always wanted to fit in and tried to change myself, or change the people around me. Then, three years ago, I was told I might die. This transformed me. I no longer wanted to be the man in the middle; the one who sits, listens, and takes in all the shitty things others think and say about the people I love and care for. I started to stand up for myself, my values and what I believe in.

Being so close to death has been a homecoming for me. Since then, I've re-embarked on my journey of self-discovery. I want to learn about myself and get to know who I really am. I want to be honest with myself and the people around me, and do whatever it takes to carry on speaking my truth and having my voice heard.

I know there were times in my life where I or someone else fucked up and yet I chose to stay in those relationships. So, for me, it's a road of discovery as I'm learning how my own past behaviours prevented me from having the relationship I want and deserve. What drives me is the fact that, like everyone, I'm also looking for love, a feeling of self-acceptance, to be proud of who I am, to feel I am ok and to walk with confidence.

Looking back, I am thankful because I have experienced amazing success and met people I would never have mixed with... but along with all the success, there was also a feeling of not being fulfilled. A lot of people simply passed through my life and I passed through theirs. This left an emptiness behind. I'm changing that now by embracing the people who matter to me and those who touch my heart.

It is the simple things that make me happy now. I love my bed, driving my car, being around my friends and clients. I love travelling and meeting people, shaking their hands and reminding them of how valuable they are. I love laughing. I love giving and receiving love. I am creating my own family — a large, vibrant and wonderful family with people from many different cultures, backgrounds and ages.

I pray every day that my day will be a good one and that I will meet remarkable ordinary people. I ask that my day will be filled with miracles and surprises.

My life already has been so wonderful and it's getting better every day.

Dear Neil,

Hey you, I know you are waiting for some sort of sign or message from God... something that will pull you through and give you the answers you are looking for. Don't despair. I know you may think this is impossible now, but let me tell you, when you get older you will be looking good and feeling great. Trust me.

It won't be easy to get there though. Actually, you'll nearly not live past 40 twice! But it's all part of your amazing journey. So, I guess what I want to say to you handsome, is that everything is going to work out perfectly fine. The dreams you have right now will come true. All of them.

Much as you are not going to do well in your exams (you and I both know this), just do your best. Relax and have fun in school. You've worked so hard to make friends and all of them are really sweet and kind, and they adore you. Enjoy them.

I realise life's pretty shitty at home. Sadly, it won't get much better, but you'll move out soon and go to all sorts of wonderful places. You have so much to look forward in your life: You'll have a boyfriend soon!... well a few in fact and many, many lovers... ooh the boys like you; you will even be famous for a few moments...

Eventually, you will get to live your life how you want it. How brilliant is that?

Finally, I want to tell you how much I love your quiet and silent courage, and your lovely young soul. You bring such a vibrant energy and enthusiasm to the spaces you fill. Never give up.

Once you learn how to express yourself and your feelings again, you will be greatly received and respected.

Honour the patience and massive love inside yourself.

In sickness and health & till death do us part, Neil Geoffrey, I will always love you.

Neil

"Never be bullied into silence.
Never allow yourself to be made a victim.
Accept no one's definition of your life,
but define it yourself."
Harvey S. Firestone

Ronny - 38

I was born in 1973 and grew up in Berlin, where I lived until the age of 11. My parents' relationship was burdened with alcoholism, violence, abuse, confusion and anger. They eventually divorced when I was 6 or 7. My mother and I somehow managed to make a fresh start and when she met my stepdad we decided (well, they decided!) to live in the north of Germany. Despite this new beginning, my mother's relationship with my stepdad was stormy and dysfunctional, too, and they divorced when I was 14. The next few years were very tough, but added a lot of steel to my character. Again, there was plenty of alcohol, different forms of abuse and more violence.

When I turned 17, I finally had enough. My life was on the brink of crumbling to dust. I missed Berlin, wanted to finish Senior High School, go to university, and get away from the person I had become. Besides, my mother's life took a turn for the worse, again! So, I just left.

I had always known I was different — even as a child — but, as I got on in years, I just wanted the world to know that I was gay. All my (straight) friends told stories about their first kisses, dates, falling in love and starting relationships. I, on the other hand, was robbed of those experiences and never managed to establish myself as a gay teenager, which really pissed me off. Even though I attracted plenty of sexual attention, it was the 'wrong' kind of sexual attention. I was introduced to sex with adults at a very young age and even dabbled in prostitution. I guess that's why I wanted to live in Berlin again: I was 17; I was gay; I knew it would be easier to be gay in a big city; I wanted to reclaim my life!

Anyway, I started over again in Berlin, came out, and finished Senior High School. However, I left Berlin in 1997 to change my life, yet again. I wanted to see the world, meet new people, and experience different cultures. I also wanted to get away from all the drugs, the toxicity of the gay scene, and the guy I had met. I had ambitions and wanted to realize them, so I went to Miami to sort out my head, but ended up in London shortly thereafter. I also lived in Spain and Japan... London, though, is my adopted home. Travelling has become an important part of who I am, because in a weird way it locates me, it broadens my horizons, and prepares me for my next stop in life.

Recently, about three years ago, my younger brother found me on Facebook — which threw me off track a little. I hadn't kept in touch with my family and none of them knew anything about my whereabouts or even whether I was still alive or not...

He (my brother) had a lot of questions. After all, he was only 7 when I disappeared. Knowing that he is well and happy takes a great load off my mind. But, that's enough to know, for I don't wish to be drawn back into their lives again. I haven't spoken to my mother in all these years. I don't know what happened to my dad or anyone else. I choose not to know... not because I am bitter, but because I have created my own family in the past 20 years. My friends are my family!

My life has been a wonderful journey, a very painful one at times, but I am glad I left home when I was 17. I am a fighter and risk-taker, and have learnt to embrace every experience and challenge that life throws at me. I am not religious, but believe that thoughts make things happen. I am very intuitive, resourceful, pragmatic, and fun-loving... always have been and always will be. I'm not afraid to speak my mind and can be very critical. Without these 'ingredients', I would not have become the person I am today! I wouldn't have experienced the things I have experienced! I wouldn't have met the people who are in my life!

I know a lot of things went wrong when I was a child, a teenager, in my 20s, and finally in my 30s. This is especially true regarding sex and my perception of my own sexuality. Of course, there are times when I ask myself whether my experiences as a child, teenager and young gay man coloured my perception of reality and influenced certain choices I made; lifestyle choices that resulted in self-destruction, and by extension my HIV status. I was diagnosed in 2009 and since then HIV has been putting me through my paces big time. BUT, I am a fighter and didn't want to get sucked into another spiral of self-destruction, which is why I am writing these words.

I began to research HIV among gay men in urban centres, because I wanted to understand what happened to me that fateful summer. I refer to it as the summer of madness. So far, I've concluded that there are a lot of gay guys — like myself — who feel lost and disillusioned by the gay scene. Consequently, many of us surrender ourselves to the idea of contracting HIV... like it's our lot in life — something that is unavoidable.

In the HIV debate, so many contributing psycho-sociological and cultural factors come into play, and I also believe the mainstream gay scene has become so toxic that it is really difficult to find the perfect solution to prevent the rising tide of HIV from sweeping through our communities.

In my opinion, HIV is still a disease that is largely underestimated. Yes, there is a greater acceptance; it's not a death sentence anymore, and modern medicine has improved markedly... BUT it ain't no picnic either.

Because of my HIV status, I really struggle to connect sex with intimacy. There have been a lot of obstacles and challenges, and I have had to grow up and learn how to make the most of what I have got left. Sometimes, I wish I had chosen a different path, but I have accepted the fact that HIV will stay with me for the rest of my life. I don't think about the future too much, but what I do know is that I want to make a difference and change other people's lives for the better. I would have loved to read these words a few years ago... when I felt lost.

I also know there are a lot of gay men who won't be able to identify with my experience, because they have managed to become authentic gay men. The last thing I wish to do is to judge others and overgeneralise. Still, I believe that too many gay men are catching HIV nowadays, and I hope that my words and story will help others re-evaluate and reclaim their life and change it for the better. I'm saying this because I do know that my life would be different if I had made different choices and had positive role models.

I cannot change the world, but I can bring about change from below!

Dear Ronny,

I know that you're currently getting ready to leave everybody and everything behind to live your own life, become the person you'd like to be and find your true self. I also know how difficult this experience is for you. You have been planning your exit for almost 12 months and having to leave your younger brother (and your cat) behind will change your mental landscape big time.

In fact, it'll break your heart and it'll take you a very, very long time to stop feeling guilty. However, we both know that you've got to get away; it's not your job to carry the family and sacrifice your dreams and goals.

Trust me, it cannot get much worse, so get ready and take the leap; you've got nothing to lose.

You are young, healthy, streetwise, clever, determined, inquisitive, and gay. You have to live in a big city. So, go back to Berlin and make a fresh start. It'll be the perfect spring-board for whatever comes next.

The good news is that you'll realise most of your goals, travel the world, and meet wonderful people in the process.

You want to live in other countries, experience different cultures, speak five languages, dance, laugh, teach, have sex with men, travel, try new things, meet people from all over the world, be creative, do your A-Levels, get a degree, and learn as much as possible, don't you?

Well, the world is your oyster! Like I said, you'll realise most of your goals, and that should provide you with the motivation required to keep fighting, right?

However, the bad news is that you'll fall flat on your face on several occasions. I don't want you to think that everything will fall into place just like that.

There will be tears, pain, fear, disappointment, homelessness, drugs, and even prostitution. Again, it cannot get much worse than the situation you're currently in, so get ready and jump.

Oh, before I forget: There is something you want, but will never get; and something you really don't want, but will get... but you're a tough cookie, n'est-ce pas?

All I want you to know is that I admire your courage, strength, and resourcefulness.

Trust your intuition, and be patient! You'll find your way... and your true self.

I love you :-)

Ronny

THE TREE
Francois Lubbe

Now that I know your weapons
your tools
your wicked tricks
and empty promises,
I can let go.

Now that I'm not scared or frightened
of your shallow smile
and heavy blows,
fickle ways
and deceitful lies,
I claim back
my flesh,
my soul,
my past
and pride.

Now that I'm not hurting anymore
and beauty
and life
and love
is within me,
I will grow.

CHAPTER FOUR

FINDING THE WAY HOME

As gay men, we strive to survive in a world that does not fully embrace or validate us for being who we are, and therefore we gradually become disconnected with our true self.

The survival strategies that we developed to help numb and mask the pain from the past gradually become a cosy prison of contradictions and inconsistent behaviours. Eventually, many of us reach a point in our lives where we want to break free from the behaviours that are no longer satisfying or self-serving. This can be difficult, as our survival strategies and limiting beliefs become so habitual that we often mistakenly identify them as a part of our true selves.

Whilst there is always an emotionally legitimate reason for developing these strategies and beliefs, there comes a time when they are no longer appropriate and our desire to leave the cosy prison becomes much stronger than our desire to remain inside it.

Realising that our behaviours no longer serve us in the way we want them to and that we need to explore a different way of existing, happens for a variety of reasons. In some cases, an emotional breakdown or crisis leads to the desire to change our lives. The end of a relationship, losing a job, a health scare or the loss of a loved one can also trigger a need for change. For some of us, it is simply that we are finally growing up — not just physically, but emotionally and psychologically.

Having reached this stage, many gay men start to question who they truly are and what they really want from life. Some of us find ourselves in therapy, on personal development workshops, embarking on a spiritual journey, reconnecting with family members, or in some cases, separating ourselves from familiar and habitual relationships and behaviours. Ultimately, when we reach this part of our journey, we are on the cusp of finding our way home. Home, in this context, is our core self. It is the part of who we truly are that we abandoned during those formative years when it was simply too painful to proudly embrace being oddly out of place.

Finding the way home means letting go of the behaviours that chain us down. In turn, we cultivate new beliefs and strategies that don't mask or numb the pain from the past or present. It is a process of becoming more conscious of our behaviour in our everyday interactions and being more aware of responding to situations, rather than reacting to them.

The first stage of the journey back home is to acknowledge the past. This stage can't be avoided because those painful childhood experiences can only be released if their impact on our way of thinking and emotions is fully understood.

This initial stage is challenging because it brings an array of emotions to the surface like betraying a caregiver who did not lovingly embrace us for being different. We might feel that we are reinforcing the negative views we already hold about ourselves, or simply be overwhelmed by the Pandora's box of pain we are about to open. All of this can be too unbearable to imagine.

However, no matter how difficult this may seem, moving through this first stage is important. It will allow any unhealed wounds and damage from our childhoods to be repaired. This stage requires honesty and an acknowledgement of whatever happened or did not happen during our childhoods. It is easy to confuse any pain that emerges in this stage as the creation of new pain, particularly as it may feel like we are reliving the emotions of the past, in the present. This is simply remembered pain, and it is part of the releasing and letting go process. This first step towards home is inevitable for anyone who wants to move away from the constraints of the past.

Setting an intention for new behaviours and attitudes which will help cultivate a different way of being is the second stage of the journey. Each person is an expert on their own life, and it is important that these intentions are relevant to where each person is coming from and how they would like to show up in their life.

Ultimately, laying down new intentions is about ensuring that the survival strategies we employed to mask or numb the pain of our limiting beliefs are substituted with ones that encourage and nurture our true self.

The journey home is not an easy one, and unfortunately, many give up half way through self-sabotage and by returning to that cosy prison of familiar beliefs and strategies. 'Old habits die hard' and for the journey back home, this is particularly true.

In order to stay on the path of reconnecting with our true selves, it is important to find support within a community that will provide encouragement during those moments that tempt us to go back to our old habits and way of life. In some instances, our friends and family might feel threatened by our desire to live a more integrated life. This is where our intentions serve as timely reminders of our goals, and our community of supporters is there to help us stay on track.

In *Finding The Way Home*, we see how these men are travelling on the journey to uncovering their true selves. In these shared experiences, this simple message is clear: finding the way home ultimately means getting to the place where we can be our true selves without feeling that we have to develop inauthentic behaviours in order to be accepted.

Home is a place within ourselves where we can look in the mirror and say silently or out loud, 'I love myself, exactly as I am.'

"Prejudice is humanity's greatest labour-saving device;
it allows people to form opinions without troubling themselves
to search for facts."
Laurence Peter

Anton - 42

I was born in Aldershot, west of London, in 1970, and I was raised by my mother in South West London, where I lived until my late teens with my two brothers, one of whom is my twin. My other brother was two years my elder.

I have never met my dad, because he and my mother separated before I was born. Very occasionally, my dad phoned my mum, but he didn't speak to my brothers or me. My mother never encouraged any communication between us. Over the years, I have never even received a birthday card from Dad, which really hurts.

Up until my early teens, I spent many summer holidays with my grandparents, who also visited us in London at Christmas time throughout my childhood. My granddad always accompanied us whenever we went on holidays on the English South Coast with my mother. He was a very important influence in my life.

We spent a lot of time together during summer holidays at my grandparents' house in Bristol, working on his car or his allotment and building things in his garage, including a model sailing boat, which I cherished. My grandma was one person who seemed to understand my need for comfort when I was upset, and in those moments, I felt very loved. The love and stability I felt around my grandparents was a critical factor in my childhood years, especially since my mother was unable to meet my emotional needs.

My mother suffered from depression all her life, and in my early teens, she began to drink heavily. At the same time, my eldest brother began to develop personal problems including depression and anger issues, which led to him engaging in alcohol and drug abuse. Life at home became increasingly volatile and dysfunctional. The years that followed were a time of increasing, yet unvoiced, desperation and uncertainty for me. From the age of 15 onwards I moved from one job to the next, seeking security and a sense of purpose, and a place in the world — but with a growing sense of rejection from others and despair about the future.

I have often felt abused and misunderstood, both at work and at home. It felt like there was no one to turn to and talk about the issues in my life. My emotional and sexual development took a back seat, due to the other problems going on at home.

At secondary school, I achieved a reasonable level of education, but I was really just treading water, not knowing what to do with my life. There was no one to guide and encourage me. My strongest subject at school was Art, which I used as a form of self-exploration and catharsis.

My granddad died of throat cancer in mid-2007 — only a few weeks after being diagnosed. I was 17 years old, and at the time of his death I was on holiday with my mother and two brothers. We had been hoping to hear of his remission so that he could join us, as he had done in previous years. Shortly after his death, my grandma moved to a care home in London to be closer to family. Granddad's death caused me to shut off emotionally and to retreat further into myself. I remember feeling cold, empty, numb and alienated from the world. It felt as though the last hope had gone and from then on, I had to go it alone.

I had a number of jobs over the years including working in Woolworths, driving a bus, working at boarding kennels for dogs and cats, and working in a laboratory, testing blood for the Blood Transfusion Service in London.

In about 1992, my eldest brother became involved in Evangelical Christianity. He saw this as an answer to all his unhappiness and problems — including the problems of his family. Even though he never fully committed himself to the church, we were all deeply affected by this religious interest in one way or another. In the absence of my dad, my eldest brother had been thrust into the role of primary carer and role model in our home. Therefore, his religious foray led to me joining the church in 1994. However, my hidden homosexuality became a growing issue for me around Christians. I eventually left the church a few years later, after becoming intensely rebellious. I felt that if I stayed in this environment, I would lose all control of myself.

In 1997, I began to exhibit more obvious emotional problems — especially at work. I had acute low self-esteem, which I had hidden well for years. I began to develop obsessive-compulsive behaviours as well as problems with anger management.

Shortly after this, I moved into supported housing for gay men who have suffered abuse, in Battersea, London. In 1999, I suffered a nervous breakdown and was unable to continue working.

Less than a year later, in January 2000, I met my life partner at a gay coming-out group in Kings Cross. We have now been together 12 years, thanks in no small part to his love and patience, as well as the love and acceptance of his family.

Following a period of self-assessment, I went on to study Fine Art and Animation at Degree Level in Norwich. I hoped to escape the pressure and pace of London and discover a renewed direction in life. This period of study was a very difficult, but nonetheless rewarding time for me. Difficult, because of the pressures and opinions of the critical art education environment, and yet rewarding because I was able, for the most part, to focus on expressing my issues creatively. I gained a renewed impetus in the pursuit of my creative and expressive art practice.

In early 2007, my eldest brother was found dead in his room at the hostel where he was staying. The actual cause of his death was never properly determined. He was my best friend when I was young, and we shared a real kinship from an early age, until my mid-teens. As life started to fall apart at home, our relationship deteriorated. His death was a huge shock to me.

My partner has a large family including a teenage son, and a daughter who is 20. I also played a part in his son's upbringing. With the support of my partner and the experience of being part of his family, I was able to pull through the trauma of my brother's death — even though I was inconsolable at the time.

I am currently expanding my group of gay friends and working towards re-engaging in social and sports activities. I am rebuilding my confidence with a view to leading a more rewarding, sociable and authentic life. I am still unclear about my chosen career path, but my priority is to honour my authentic self, and that of others, in whatever I do. I hope to play a more assertive and confident role in whatever vocation I settle into. I want to make a contribution based on my life experience and desire to fulfil my own potential, and encourage the same in others. I also plan to get in touch with my father in the near future.

I am learning to forgive myself about the past and understand that high standards come at a high price; if I don't accept my own need to learn and grow in an authentic way, then how can I contribute and feel a sense of pride in what I do? I should seek out those who are open to at least trying, and encourage those who aren't; and that includes myself at times.

The future awaits...

Dear Anton,

I feel the need to acknowledge the things happening in your life right now, and to show that I appreciate you as a young man who deserves recognition. Before I continue though, let me say this: don't worry… I am writing to you because I see that you need some affirmation and support through this very difficult time.

I see your personal struggle and I wish to honour your courage in that — which is clearly evident! Hopefully this letter will serve as a valuable reminder of your strengths, which are a resource that will serve you well on your journey, and into your future.

There is no judgement or blame attached to what I will be saying — for absolutely anything! This letter is for your benefit — no one else's!

We all struggle through teenage life — even when things are apparently normal — but when they are chaotic and uncertain, as they are in your life right now, it's a lot tougher to cope with. So be patient, kind and gentle with yourself.

I truly believe that you will endure what you are going through right now and that you will have a fine future as a mature and conscientious man.

So here goes, Anton…

I see that you are angry with Mum for her selfish and contradictory behaviour towards you. Her lack of sensitivity to your feelings and needs, and how she disregards you in front of others, leaves you totally aghast, confused and frustrated. One minute she is trying to show she loves you and the next she is pushing you away. This behaviour really hurts you and you don't know how to express this pain. If you try to talk to Mum about it, you know she will deny and reject your 'truth'.

This adds to your feelings of invalidation and anger and you feel really abused by this. Inside you are still a child, who has needs, and you should not have to deal with Mum's problems. But remember Mum's behaviour is no reflection on you! It is rooted in her own denial, and unresolved pain and fear around her own needs.

The fact that Mum and your eldest brother fight aggravates matters at home a lot. Mum blames him for her unhappiness and frustration because he is male, and she believes he is "just like your father". She keeps shoving all the blame and baggage of what happened between her and dad in his direction. She is wrong for doing this. How she views men is no reflection on you or your brother.

All the blaming and fighting at home leaves you feeling scared and abandoned. The situation is also very difficult for you because you feel an obligation to defend Mum when your brother gets angry with her. Yet, you also feel a deep love and protectiveness for your brother and you feel guilty about having to choose sides.

I assure you, Anton, having to take sides between two people you really love and care about will make anyone feel torn, helpless and angry. These are valid feelings and you shouldn't punish yourself for having them.

It is understandable that you defend Mum. Don't blame yourself for this. If anything, this demonstrates Mum's lack of understanding of her role in the situation. She cannot accept responsibility for her actions, or inactions, and is unable to meet the needs of her boys.

Your older brother is not coping well either — with the arguments and difficult home life. The pressure he is under is beginning to cause him personal problems, and the blame he gets from Mum is contributing to his heavy drinking. You are witnessing his problems escalating with his growing anger. You used to look up to him for support and guidance, but because you are so close to him, you are afraid that you will get caught up in the middle of what he has to deal with.

In the past, you had such a great affinity with your older brother — but now you feel frightened of him. The direction his life is taking scares you, which adds to your feelings of vulnerability and anger. You are afraid you will lose his friendship, love and support, which you have come to value and depend on so much. You know it's not his fault that things are going the wrong way for him, so it's hard for you to express your feelings without guilt and without wanting to defend yourself with anger and blame.

You feel you have not been supportive towards your brother — knowing he has meant so much to you in the past — and yet you are angry with him. There is no one to blame. Yet, in some strange way, you feel responsible for him. You love him and want to help him and show how much you appreciate his always being there for you, but your own worries and fears are preventing you from doing this. This guilt is a real burden for you, because you see that he is slipping away from you and you have no power to stop it from happening.

The chaos and conflict at home are terrifying. The fights and angry outbursts have turned your life into a living hell, and you justifiably fear the collapse of your family. You really want to get out — but you also fear being on your own and that you won't cope.

You wish Mum could show you the love you need — rather than trying to compensate for her inadequacies by telling you she does, yet she is not demonstrating it. Unfortunately, she has her own unresolved issues and is selfishly wrapped up in these. This affects you profoundly. She is unable to express the love and recognition that you absolutely and necessarily need her to — so she is emotionally unavailable to you.

One thing is certain though: she is indisputably attached to you — as you are to her. I know this attachment is something that you really want to break away from because it is painful and confusing. You feel stuck, angry and abused.

Mum wants you to know that she loves you — but you don't believe this because of her selfish behaviour and because you feel so rejected by this. She is projecting her issues and needs outwards onto you, rather than acknowledging you and meeting your real needs in the here and now. No wonder you feel unseen and unheard. Remember that Mum behaves like this because she is unable to love and accept herself.

Try to see her for who she truly is and what she cannot be for you — and learn to accept that. You rightfully feel that you must protect yourself from Mum. Her words of love are not followed through with actions of support and care. However, here's a word of warning: don't resent her for who she is. It will only destroy you!

It's perfectly understandable that you think the only way to cope under these circumstances is to go it alone. People can misunderstand this and be unkind, but learn to stay focused on your needs and remain strong in this. Do not empathize with Mum at the cost of your own happiness, and don't feel guilty for having needs of your own. Stick to your goal of wanting to find stability and fulfilment, aiming to be mature and whole, and try not to take setbacks to heart. Eventually you will find the contentment you deserve - this goal will help you to endure what is happening at home.

I see your sadness. I see that you are searching for an honourable role in life and a true identity... and all this in the absence of good role models. No wonder you sometimes think you don't fit into the world around you. You feel a lot of pressure because you have no one to guide and support you right now. I can see that you feel very lonely and you are asking yourself "how long can I cope with this?".

Right now, you are struggling to keep your head above water and at times you feel you are fit to burst! You are confused, full of self-doubt and anger, and you feel imprisoned and stuck. I see how your fears and doubts about the future are taking hold of you. Trying so hard to earn your worth, without the love and support you need is something you should guard against — for your own protection. You may not understand everything right now or the reasons why you have to go through this, and it's hard not knowing what the solution is. However, in time, these experiences will be what builds your commitment and passion for what is right and true — so be patient with yourself.

I see that you need comfort, reassurance, support and direction, but you are unsure of where to get it from, or even what it looks like. I know you don't ask for help because you are afraid to risk more pain and disappointment. As a result, you withdraw from who you really are and look for a way to escape from the pain, confusion and guilt. But take heart, you have worthy emotional instincts even though others don't always appreciate or understand this.

You keep your emotions in close check because there is so much you cannot control right now, which is scary, and you are so much in need of emotional security and a calmer, less volatile existence. To express your feelings and anger seems dangerous and impossible, and so you contain them because you fear something dreadful might happen if you let go.

Sometimes we take refuge to preserve our hearts and minds by hiding and staying silent. We do this out of care for ourselves. However, there are circumstances when we must speak out and show our true selves. This can be painful at times, and we don't always get the understanding we hope for and often deserve.

Make it your goal to preserve, but also share, the hidden child within you with people whom you have taken the time to learn to trust and those who will show you respect. This is vital and you will need this contact now more than at any other time in your life. Make the effort to find like-minded friends — perhaps those with similar struggles. Share your hardship and concerns with them, and take courage from their comradeship. I know you find this hard, but open up to those people because it is an opportunity to gain strength from their support.

Luckily, there are people you can turn to and places you can go to get help. No one will get into trouble if you ask for this support. I know you worry about that, but you can keep the personal details anonymous if you wish, to protect those you love. So I urge you to find people you can talk to — for your own sake. This will assist you to cope with what life throws at you and you will be less likely to do things that you may regret in the future.

You will gain a lot of strength if you honour the feelings that make you human.

Value all of yourself... even the parts you feel are unlikeable. You are not bad or wrong as you are. It's just a very difficult time for a sensitive young man who is looking for direction and hope. You are trying so hard to do the right thing and behave in a way that is respectful and doesn't offend or hurt anyone. But you seem to forget that you yourself are feeling very hurt inside and misunderstood a lot of the time.

I really admire you for being so brave and strong. You are a loving and kind individual who is really trying to do well, but this is just too much to cope with right now, especially when you are going it alone! So be kind to yourself and continue to be courageous. You can and will survive this!

Remember there is no shame in what is happening at home.

The wonderful thing is that you still have such a great love and enthusiasm for life – this is truly who you are and it is these qualities that give you so much strength.

Right now I guess it's very hard to see a light at the end of the tunnel. But you have the power within you — right now! — to shine a light on everything that surrounds you. You will find a path through the pain and confusion, and you will discover the best thing to do — for you — and your family — now and in the future.

I see your courage and your desire for honesty and openness. Remember courage is to experience fear and step up to the challenge anyway. It's not to be without fear but to conquer it. You have already proven so far that you can do this — many times.

Finally, you deserve to be loved and respected, and to love and respect yourself. Share your true self with others and life will become a limitless experience of affirmation.

All my love,

Anton X

"It's a long walk from the dressing room to the stage."
Patti LuPone

Blake - 36

I was born in South Africa but shortly afterwards moved to the United Kingdom. After a certain period my family moved back to South Africa, where I was exposed, over a long period of time, to the racist, elitist, white supremacy and homophobia of the previous South African apartheid regime. This came as a huge shock compared to the dynamic and cultural melting pot of London.

As a child, I suffered with congenital cataracts and had to undergo several eye operations. As a result, I had to wear thick glasses, which resulted in much bullying and teasing. Years later, I finally had artificial implants in my eyes, which improved my eyesight and ended a lot of the bullying and teasing.

Much to the chagrin of my family, I became heavily involved in an Evangelical Christian church. At the same time, I was in training as a professional actor, which alongside my church activities, gave me my fair share of troubles. I eventually attended an ex-gay ministry, called *Living Waters*, which was a six-month weekly course aiming to "heal the issue of same sex attraction".

This brought up many issues, which eventually contributed to me having a major depressive episode, where I experienced suicidal thoughts. It eventually came to be that I had to look honestly at the Bible in context, and accept that being gay is not an issue before God, and that coming out as openly gay was a matter of honest survival. I am now attending an inclusive Anglican church and I am back in London, pursuing my acting career in full force. Learning to accept myself has been the biggest challenge so far, but one that helps me grow day by day.

Dear Blake,

I need to be honest and upfront with you. You are not a freak and you are not an outcast. You are talented, funny, witty, driven, attractive and a courageous young man with a sharp mind, a good heart and you are not in any way a mistake.

You have tried for years to conceal that you are gay. Don't worry about it. You being gay does not equal mental illness, a disorder or being a wannabe paedophile. You are not cursed by God and there is nothing wrong with you. You do not have to be perfect or in any way make yourself more than what you already are. You are okay, just the way you are.

The 'church people' who will ostracise you and avoid you, will feel threatened by you, be afraid of your honesty and directness, are not to be taken notice of. Keep being who you are and do not be ashamed of your insights and your thoughts. Never allow anyone to demand that you give up your ability to reason, your sense of self and your personal power. You are a gift to many people and will be to many more. I repeat: you are not a mistake.

Shine and allow yourself to be who you are. You being gay is only one aspect of the amazing and beautiful person you are. No ostracism, abuse or shame dumped on you by your family can ever take your worth away. Walk with confidence, because you have nothing to be scared of.

You will encounter ex-gay groups who will try to change you. My advice is to politely, but absolutely firmly, tell them you are not interested and want nothing to do with the ex-gay movement. They should know that God loves you as you are. If they become hostile or vindictive - walk away. Most of the biggest homophobic people are secretly gay or fearful of their own impulses. So, ignore their crazy rants. In time you will see the wheels come off their ridiculous theories and you'll realise that their bigoted narrow-minded views have very little to do with God and what they say and do only brings harm to others.

Follow your dreams. You can succeed. You want to be a lead actor? Then do it! You are allowed to enjoy your life and be happy. Remember, you are not a mistake.

With love,

Blake

"I love that I was never meant to fit in or to be the same as everyone else. I love life and don't resent being here."

David

David - 48

I was born in December 1963, and spent the first 19 years of my life in Pembroke, a small town in West Wales. My father was a doctor and my mother a housewife. Both were raging alcoholics by the time I came along.

Life felt very unstable to me. There was a huge amount of violence between my parents. I believed my mother would die at the hands of my father. I made him the villain, and her the victim. This wasn't actually the case, but it was how things looked to me as a very young child. I felt that I had to protect her, but couldn't, and was ashamed of this; inadequate in my masculinity. These were my very early preoccupations.

I was raped by an uncle at around the age of 3, an experience that continued over a period of years. This had a huge impact on my life. Adult sexual energy in a young child's body overloaded the delicate circuits and blew most of the fuses. I was completely scrambled and running on sexual energy.

Until the age of 10, I had quite a lot of sex with men and older boys. When I reached puberty the sex stopped, for the most part. I just masturbated ferociously, and I fell in love with unobtainable straight boys.

I knew I was different, always felt that I didn't fit, didn't belong, and, of course, there was nothing I wanted more. I believed my only option was to pretend, to deny huge parts of my reality, in order to be accepted. I became a convincing actor, but felt a very deep sense of shame, and inadequacy. I hated myself, and believed that on the inside, I was ugly and wrong.

I followed in the family tradition: not medicine, but addiction, and knew I was an alcoholic by the time I was 15. I was a reasonably intelligent kid, but had stopped trying by the time I was 14. I had no idea that I was furious, really angry, confused and hurt. I just knew that I was wrong, and nothing I could do would 'fix' things for me. I had no understanding that living a gay lifestyle was an option, but as soon as I came to London, when I was 19, a new world opened up to me. This was in 1983. AIDS had recently surfaced.

I made it my mission to have as much sex as possible, and to thoroughly explore my sexuality. This obviously went hand in hand with huge amounts of drink and drugs. A lifestyle of self-destruction ensued. I didn't study, had a series of dead-end jobs, and was always terrified on the inside, on the run from some unnameable anxiety and a well of shame.

I contracted HIV in September 1992. In those days it was a death sentence, and my doctor told me this in no uncertain terms. I resorted to my old ways of coping — drinking more alcohol, taking drugs and having sex. By this stage, there were other things too, but none was as important as these were.

Gardening started to feature in my life again, something I had always loved, even as a child. An internal sense of spirituality had also started to emerge at the end of the 80s.

A strengthening of intuition, direct guidance, seeing and hearing things that I couldn't rationalise. These were all experiences I frequently had as a child, and here they were again, in the midst of my addictive, chaotic lifestyle.

I couldn't accept the beauty and love I was experiencing on the inside, as a result of these experiences, so I worked even harder to destroy it. I tried to drown it out. It was desperately painful. My self-hatred was being pushed to the surface by the emergence of something much more valid and true.

Eventually, I stopped using drugs, and was in immediate crisis. I had liver cancer. It was a superb and dramatic turning point in my life... I'm always one to enjoy a bit of drama. I was told I wouldn't survive the cancer and I had to make one of those stark decisions.

Live or die. What was it going to be?

I realised I had always been trying to die; I spent a lifetime not showing up and here I was, about to exit this body permanently. Was that really what I wanted?

I chose to live. Much as I was tempted by death, I chose life. The cancer disappeared. I thought once the cancer was gone, life would be hunky-dory but it wasn't, because the shit I buried and avoided hit the surface, and I had to wade through it all.

Now, towards the end of my forties, I can say I am happy. I love and accept myself.

I don't resent each new day. I have studied garden design, and am training in Permaculture — an ethical framework for living lightly on the planet, and making sure that we can sustain human activities for many generations to come, in harmony with nature. I work consciously with my spirituality, and help others do the same. The intuitive awareness that I have is utilised in my work with gardens, plants, people, animals and places.

I am no longer led through my life by my sexual appetite, or by a desire to avoid as much pain as possible. Instead, I am led by my heart, which opens to more joy than I used to think was allowed.

I am learning that there are no limits to the abundance and beauty of life.

Dear David,

I want more than anything to tell you that I am proud of you, I am really proud. I love you, very much.

I am proud of your strength and your courage. You have already faced things in your life that many children of your age will never have to experience. I am proud of the fact that you have survived, and have a great sense of humour.

At this present moment, I know you feel that there is no one who understands, no one you can turn to and that even though you have a good group of friends, you feel terribly alone. It won't always be that way.

I also know that you live in fear of people knowing that you are gay, and that you believe that your only option would be to kill yourself, if the people in your town found out about your secret.

That's a huge burden you carry. You probably won't believe me, but what you think and feel is not the truth: what you constantly tell yourself about your friends and family, "If only they knew the real me, they would hate and despise me", that's not reality. You are liked for who you are, and for the many admirable qualities you do have.

When, in the future, these friends know about your sexuality, they will still love you, and so will your family.

Loving men and wanting to have sex with men is not the shameful thing you are being told it is. You will grow into a world where it is possible to be happy, open, express your sexuality freely, and choose whomever you want to love. Your deep sensitivity that you are so ashamed of and that you try desperately to hide because you think it will give you away, is one of your greatest strengths. Nurture it if you can. Hold on to it.

Trust your intuitions about people, places and things. This will bring you great satisfaction, as it will keep you in touch with what is true and natural within you, even when you feel that everything you do and say is a lie. By the way, it isn't: you're just doing what you need to do to get by, and that's ok; it's creative, and inventive.

It's ok to be angry and hurt at some of the things you have experienced. That's natural. It's also ok to ask for help. You don't actually have to go through life believing that there is no help available and you have to do it all on your own. Reach out, ask for help. You're going through a lot, and it doesn't make much sense.

You are precious, and funny and brave. We didn't choose supportive or available parents this time, so I say these things to you, because no one else is, and you need to hear this: who and what you are is beautiful, and wise, capable and strong. Believe in yourself, trust yourself. You're not wrong. You're not a design fault, and you're not meant to be the same as everyone else. Let go of wishing you had never been born, or thinking you should have been different.

You are all right, just as you are.

You may not understand this, but I'm going to say it anyway:

From where I stand now, I send a ribbon, a line of light and energy back through time (yes, that's possible), to you where you are. I anchor it in your heart. This ribbon is there to give you strength and courage, to give you something to hold on to and to remind that you are always loved.

Trust this ribbon of light to guide you from the inside, to a bright future.

I will say this one more time, because you need to hear this: I am proud of you and I love you so very much.

David

xxx

"Freedom lies in controlling one's emotions."
Anonymous

Daniel - 47

I was born in the mid-sixties in a nice city in the south of Spain. Since I can remember, I have always been gay. My first sexual encounter was at the age of 10 when I fooled around with a guy four years older than me. I went to a Catholic school for 10 years and I remember being bullied by a bunch of guys. Although I don't think this was because I was gay, it still made a really big impact on my life.

I never had any problem with my sexuality. I actually accepted it bit by bit, as I grew up. From a very young age, I learned how to cope with living two lives. The one where I was expected to go out with the most beautiful girls to prove that I was 'that' macho man, and my other life, the one that I was proud to be living, when I used to leave those girls at home and go to places where I could meet with people of my own kind.

I used to see myself as the typical comic book hero with two lives, and I realised very early in my life that I would never get married or have children. All of this was happening at a steady pace and I accepted myself as I got older.

Once I left school, I moved to another city with the excuse that I couldn't study for my career in the city where I grew up. However, my real purpose was to live my own 'different' life and to leave my family behind so they wouldn't be affected by it. I also left because the first love of my life was in the city where I wanted to study. I spent five and a half years with him.

As I grew older, I was more aware and proud of my sexuality and I use to share my secret with people whom I thought at the time were appropriate. One day my parents came to visit me in my new city and a family member told them, in a very bad way, that I was gay and I was living with a man. My parents were completely devastated, especially my father. He was a very important bank director, who was well known for his affairs with the most beautiful women before he married my mother.

The worst thing in this world that you could do to my father was to give him a gay son. I automatically passed from being the most important person in his life to being the most disgusting thing in the world. I agreed to see a psychologist who, instead of dealing with "my problem", actually tried to calm my parents down. This didn't last. My relationship with my father went from being a very good one to fighting continuously with him. It was a very difficult time and I remember feeling stressed and anxious all the time.

Soon after that, my father got ill with pulmonary fibrosis and played on my feelings by making me feel guilty about his illness and saying that I would be the cause of his death. Some time after this he died in my arms, and I was the last person that he saw. The situation between us remained unresolved.

I have an amazing mother. She was overshadowed by my father's perception of gay people. She once defended me against my father by explaining to him that if being gay was a fault, like not having an arm, then she would still love me. It wasn't until my father died that she started having her own and more positive ideas about homosexuality. Today, she is the best thing I have in my life.

My second relationship was with an English man who lived in Spain at that time. In the beginning everything was fun and great. He proposed to me to have an open relationship, I didn't know what that was, but it felt interesting, fresh and most of all different and modern. I agreed and we had a great time living together and having sex with other men. But then, I completely fell in love with him and something that started out to be fresh and modern turned into jealousy and pain.

I didn't know how to manage that pain. I wanted to tell him that I didn't want an open relationship, but I felt that I had signed something, and by un-signing it, I would show him my weakness and hence he would leave me. On the other hand, I couldn't cope with seeing him with others, so my behaviour was very chaotic and we ended the relationship after having many problems. I don't think he ever realised any of this.

Later, I decided to move to London, where I had a lot of fun during my first years there. I met my third boyfriend, an ex-married man with children. We fell in love and at one point, I decided to take the big step of taking him to Spain to introduce him to my mother. Once we were there, his behaviour completely changed towards me. I tried to understand what was happening, but he continued with the same attitude. I got very angry with the situation and tried to talk to him to resolve it, but he didn't talk at all and with no explanation, he left me there in Spain.

Afterwards, back in London, a series of encounters followed with him where I allowed him to play with my feelings, to confuse me and to hurt me. This caused me to fall into a very deep depression, which lasted for more than two years.

Most of my encounters with the men I loved have left me with this sense of abandonment; it seems like a pattern, like a curse, like unfinished business with the first man that I loved, my father.

Now I am 47 years old, and I feel as if all of the pieces of my life experience are like tiles spread on the floor. I see them, I understand them, but the most difficult thing now is that I have to rearrange, and put them back together, in order for me to be myself again.

Dear Daniel,

You have to understand that it is very difficult for Dad to accept that you are gay. If he is angry with you, it is because he loves you very much and if you are angry with him, it is for exactly the same reason.

Do not fight back at him emotionally blackmailing you. It is his only weapon and the only way for him to cope with this difficult situation. Put yourself in his shoes, and feel his pain and understand his behaviour. Then sit in front of him and be as honest as you can be.

Tell him these three things:

1. Being gay is not an option. It is not something that you choose, like the colour of your hair. It is not your fault, it's not Dad's fault, it is nobody else's fault. In fact, it isn't actually a fault at all.

2. Being gay is not an illness. It is a way of being and it cannot be "cured". No matter how hard you try, you cannot change it or reverse it.

3. But most important of all, and probably the most difficult to accept, is that you are happy being gay and that it is not something that you want to change, so there is no need for him to worry about you. Tell him that you will be OK.

Essentially, it does not matter how difficult it is for anyone. If being gay is not an option, if it is nobody's fault, if it cannot be changed and most of all, if you are happy, the only thing for everyone to do is to accept it and embrace it... Dad must accept you!

If Dad is worried about other people's reactions, promise him that you will never put him in any difficult situation.

And remember one thing, in human relationships, where there is pain, it is always because there is love.

Love,

Daniel

*"The present is a good place to be in,
since you never know what gifts you
are going to receive...
That's why it's called the present."*

Grand Master Oogway — KungFu Panda

Tyrone - 45

I've known from a young age that I was gay. My first experience was when I was young (around 8) and I just kept it as my little secret.

I grew up in a very religious family — Seventh Day Adventists — and we went to church every Saturday. This religious environment made my life hell, because I was not like the other boys; always helping my mum and trying to pretend that I was straight. When I decided to leave the church, I felt relieved not to have to hide or lie about who I was anymore.

Things were very similar at school, because my 'secret' was used against me and I was picked on and bullied by the other kids. It left me hating myself for being gay. I had a lot of cooped-up anger and also became very withdrawn.

My upbringing, things that happened at home and the way I was treated in school had a massive impact on how I saw relationships and love. Since I was considered to be weak, I started to believe this. As a result, I put up with a lot of abuse from boyfriends, who mistreated me both physically and emotionally.

Looking back, I know my life has certainly had its ups and downs, but through it all, I survived and become stronger. I finally feel that I am going somewhere with my life. I'm working in a job that I enjoy. I'm taking better care of myself and make a real effort to be proactive. I've also started to look into my past and confront the issues that I have avoided in the past. This is an on-going process for me, but I have realised that in order to move forward in life, I have to defy the things that keep me back.

I am learning to love and respect myself. I now know that we are all special in our very own way and there's no reason for me, or anybody else for that matter, to believe anything different.

Dear Tyrone,

I know you are going through a lot and you may feel scared. Please, please don't let anyone tell you that you are not worthy. You are strong, good looking and have a lot to give.

Life is going to be hard, but you will overcome your difficulties. However, this is very important: you can say 'No' and you don't ever have to put up with shit.

You are smart, bright and very caring. Don't let anybody ever hurt or abuse you. Always fight back. Not with your fists, but with the knowledge that you are strong. Open up to other people and believe in your dreams.

Be open to new ideas and experiences. Go on holidays and see more of the world... you will love it! Love yourself and remember it's okay to say 'No'.

Love,

Tyrone

"You can accept or reject the way you are treated by other people, but until you heal the wounds of the past, you will continue to bleed. You can bandage the bleeding with food, with alcohol, with drugs, with work, with cigarettes, with sex, but eventually it will ooze through and stain your life.

You must find the strenght to open the wounds, stick your hands inside, pull out the core of the pain that is holding you in your past, the memories, and make peace with them. "
Iyanla Vanzant

Francois - 37

The first nine years of my life were spent in a small industrial town called Boksburg, in South Africa. We lost my father when I was 2 years old, on New Year's Eve, 1976. He died of a heart attack, aged 32. I don't remember anything about him. My mother never spoke about him and the only testimony I have of his character was from my grandmother, who fondly told me that he was a good man with a great sense of humour. I used to look at photographs of him, wondering if I would be as handsome as he was when I grew up.

In the late 1970s, in a stiflingly religious, puritan, and racist South Africa, the fate of a young widow was similar to that of a divorcée. It was the baby booming era and few men were prepared to raise another man's children. So to say that life was tough after my father's death, would be an understatement. My mother often said to us: "Because of you two I won't get married again." Those words and the fact that she was a young beautiful, lonely woman made me feel responsible for her happiness and I tried my best to be a 'good boy'. I failed. I often found her crying in her room and on particularly bad days, she paced up and down the hall, cursing into the skies calling to my dad, saying: "And you leave me with this!"

I saw how my mother was traumatised by the many boyfriends coming and going in and out of her life. I put it on myself to 'protect' her from hurting. As a result, I became hostile towards men — in particular those who showed a romantic interest in my mother. In my reality, I was the man of the house, despite the fact that I was the youngest. My trying to be 'Dad' infuriated my brother and he retaliated by bullying me. If I think about it now, I suppose he was just trying to stand his own ground and wanted to be valued in his own way.

My mother worked full-time in a laboratory at a sewage farm — a job she hated, not just because of the stench, but also because it barely paid the bills. There was always a sense of 'not having enough', and I felt that she would've been better off without us and that my brother and I had taken everything away from her. Being a single parent and working full-time left my mother tired and depressed, and she used her weekends to rest and recover. So she didn't always have the energy or inclination to spend time with me and my brother. This left both of us with a sense of not being loved and deprived of the attention any child deserves.

Despite these difficulties, there were also good times. My best friend, Jonathan, and I were nicknamed 'David and Jonathan' — a reference to the brotherly love between the biblical characters David and Jonathan. We were inseparable. Jonathan's mother Lydia was like a second mother to me. She understood my needs and gave my mother much-needed support and sisterly love. Especially since I later learned that it was difficult for my mother to be completely honest with her real family about the difficulties she faced.

My fondest memories are of our family gatherings over Christmas and New Year. Being together like that gave me such a sense of comfort and security. My brother and I fought less, and my mother seemed more peaceful and even made time to play with us. It was great fun to visit my aunt (my mother's only sister) and her husband, and I adored my two cousins who I treated like my own sisters. For me, they were the perfect family and something I wanted to be a part of. My aunt gave me a paint set and brushes, and encouraged me to draw and write; she was much gentler than my mother was. My uncle taught me how to ride a bike and he took my brother and me on fishing trips. In fact, apart from my grandfather, he was the only man I really trusted because he was kind and caring, and showed a genuine interest in my wellbeing.

I revelled in the holidays we spent with my grandparents. I spent a lot of time with my grandmother in her sewing room, where she taught me how to use a needle and a thread, and showed me how to make dolls' clothes and sew buttons on shirts. I loved baking with her and often wrote down my own extravagant pretend recipes for salads and cakes — none of which would've been edible. My granddad was an amazing carpenter — a skill he taught me. I helped him build a grandfather clock, furniture and a few dolls' houses for my cousins. Of course, I also completely indulged myself by decorating them once they were finished.

Playing with other boys scared me as a result of my brother's bullying and the complexities of how I viewed men in general. If I wasn't with Jonathan, I was on my own. Lost in my own little fantasy world. I dressed up in my mother's dresses and shoes and walked up to the quarry in the field behind our house where people dumped their old cars, rusty refrigerators and bric-à-brac. I often dismantled car doors and seats and carried them back to our house where I would build a den — to my mother's dismay — on the front lawn. Back then, my creativity and little eccentricities were tolerated and no one made fun of me or said anything to make me feel bad about my behaviour. In this sense, my childhood was amazing.

I grew up in a Christian fundamentalist environment where people went to church — sometimes twice on a Sunday — and God was someone we all feared. He was the go-to-guy who had the ability to redeem us from all our human 'badness'. He was supposed to be a rainmaker in times of droughts and the only one that could fix any problem. However, unanswered prayers meant that you did something wrong in the eyes of God and weren't ready to be pardoned for your sins... which resulted in more prayer and more church.

I used to barter with God in my prayers and often offered my mother's silver tray and tea set — which I thought was very valuable — as a payoff for Him answering my prayers. My negotiation with Him did not pay off; He did not make us rich, neither did He make my mother happy or gave me my dad back and nor did He make my brother stop bullying me.

When I was seven and a half, the emotional and financial stress at home sent my mother into a slow downward spiral. Her health deteriorated. She had chronic asthma which in her eyes was a weakness, and similar to all other challenges in her life she was too stubborn to accept any help.Though she had a few bad asthma attacks in the past, they now became more frequent and more severe. She lost consciousness at least twice at home and had to be rushed to hospital. She often said: "I will never see 40." This frightened me and I was scared that something would happen to her.

Our home environment became toxic. I turned into a weepy, clingy and needy little boy which only drove my mother further away from me. She behaved more erratically, being loving and happy one moment, changing to anger and melancholy the next. This made me anxious. I wet my bed almost every night, cried a lot and did not want to go to school or leave her side. At the same time, I was uncertain of how she would react to me. It happened that a few times I ended up on the wrong side of her temper.

My mother died when I was 9 years old. It was a Saturday. She was 37. I was alone at home with her when it happened.

My mother's sister became our legal guardian. She and my uncle were both very young when they took us into their home and as much as I wanted to embrace my new family, adjusting to my new circumstances was very difficult. In the beginning, my aunt and uncle made a great effort to give us a safe and loving home. However, my brother refused to accept my aunt as his caregiver, which made things very difficult for her. I know she felt a tremendous duty to do her best for us and honour my mother. Even though I loved my aunt, I was torn between choosing her and betraying my brother, and worst, my own mother. My brother blamed me for my mother's death and his bullying increased in what I guess was a projection of his own feelings of insecurity and displacement. He also terrorized my cousins. This was his way of showing everyone that he was the big brother. Sadly, this behaviour estranged him from the rest of us. As an adult I have not spoken to him for years and I don't know where he is in the world.

Within a few weeks of my mother's death, in a very sincere display of being my protector, my brother gave me a little book. He said that my mother would've wanted me to read it. The little purple booklet *What every boy wants to know*, was discovered by my aunt in the top of my cupboard and all hell broke loose. Given that I was not even 10 years old, learning about the birds and the bees was probably a bit early for me... and if I'm honest, the drawings inside terrified me and I hardly understood what I saw. The only message I got from this experience was that sex was 'wrong' and something to be ashamed of. It was the only sex education I ever received in my life.

Tensions were mounting in our new family as I had great difficulty accepting my uncle as the man of the house. By now, I was conditioned to believe that men could not be trusted and even though I loved my uncle, our relationship was not running smoothly as a father and son. I soon learned that I was not the son he had hoped for. I was not allowed to play with dolls, or in the dolls house with my cousins and I once got a walloping for walking around in high heeled shoes. Instead, my uncle wanted me to be tough and was dead set on turning me into a man. My eccentricities and creativity were something he did not understand. As a result, my once wonderful, loving and caring uncle became my enemy; another man who disappointed and frightened me.

I am mindful of the fact that my new family was also trying to deal with my mother's death. They also lost someone who was very near and dear to them. However, being such young parents themselves, my aunt and uncle were not equipped for the task laid before them. Instead of allowing us to grieve and mourn our loss, we all went for family counselling in an effort to deal with our collective trauma and to establish clearly defined roles within the family. Unfortunately, the counselling was not successful. It was a frustrating situation for everyone, and my aunt behaved a few times in the similar explosive way that my mother did. I often felt that I was no better off with my stepmom than I was with my mother. But I have forgiven my her for this because she had the best intentions of being a good guardian and me making her feel second best and not good enough as a parent, affected her deeply.

When I was 13, I was sent to a horrible boarding school that was notoriously run like a military institution. Here the other boys nicknamed me Liberace which at first I thought was a compliment, but soon realised it was the beginning of much harsher ridicule that would follow. Being bullied and assaulted for being 'different' and 'weird' happened almost daily. By now, I knew that I was attracted to boys, and I tried to do everything in my power to hide it... especially in the showers, where it proved most difficult.

Once my secret was discovered, the teasing and physical abuse got worse. At night, the older boys burned my feet with cigarette lighters while I was asleep or they simply beat the crap out of me. I was a late developer and sometimes they ordered me to one of their rooms, where they made me strip down naked and teased me because I had no pubic hair. One afternoon they made me stand against a wall along with four other oddballs, and hurled bricks at us. If we tried to dodge the flying bricks, they threatened to beat us... I lived in constant fear and started to suffer with bulimia and trichotillomania — the compulsive urge to pull out one's own hair because of anxiety and stress.

I begged my step-parents to put me in a different school, but because I was too embarrassed and ashamed to tell them why I suffered so much torment, they thought I was simply looking for attention and making up excuses. Instead of helping me, they made the empty promise of reconsidering my request if things got worse. I lived in this false hope for three years and finally realised that my aunt and uncle had no intention of removing me from boarding school. I felt betrayed.

Not being able to confide freely in them broke all residual trust I had in my adoptive parents. At school, I felt fearful and abandoned, and at home, I felt isolated, alone and unloved. My grades dropped and at the age of 15 I was diagnosed with depression. I saw a few psychologists, all of whom had a very religious approach with their therapy — God and Prozac were obviously the answers to all my problems. I withdrew completely from my caregivers and my cousins, and I stopped making any effort to engage with the people at home. My relationship with my grandparents started to fall apart too. I became a moody, brooding, depressed and rebellious teenager.

Aged 16, it dawned on me that I had to fend for myself in the world. I figured that if I made myself useful to the older boys in boarding school, they would leave me alone. One of my hobbies as a young boy was to groom and the cut the hair of our poodle Fluffy. Using this 'experience', I started cutting hair and became the boarding school's resident hairdresser which turned out to be a handy little money-spinner. The bullying stopped and I even made friends with the same guys who used to torment me.

Soon I became the boy the other guys asked for fashion advice and tips on keeping their girlfriends happy... Of course, now that I was the 'cool' crowd's 'mascot', I also had to have my own girlfriend. Luckily, my popularity grew as the creative, funny and rebellious guy, so I had no problem hooking up with girls. I also managed to keep my desires intact in the shower, which stopped any rumours about me being a 'bum chum' and 'poofter.'

Still, the mixed messages about sexuality and sex were persisted. I knew being gay was unacceptable and my efforts to show that I was normal failed. The girlfriends I introduced to my stepmom did not win her approval. This made it difficult for me to fathom what would please her and I started to fear that I would never be able to find someone to love. Apart from that, kissing girls was horrible. I didn't like the way they tasted and attempting to fondle their breasts provided more amusement than pleasure which didn't go down well with them as you can imagine.

Over weekends, when I visited home, I routinely went to the library, where I spent hours looking at photographs of David Bowie and Mick Jagger dressed in tight jeans or spandex Glam Rock costumes. I once found a Spartacus gay travel guide and tore out some of pictures of half-naked men. Back at home, I hid those pictures in a record album sleeve. I lived in constant fear that they would be discovered. Deep down I hoped that my attraction to men was just a phase. It was in the 80s and the AIDS epidemic sent shockwaves through the world; the media and church sent clear messages that gay people were sinful outcasts and that they all would die a horrible death. So I nurtured my secret quietly and in moments of guilt, I desperately bartered with God to spare me from living an awful and shameful life.

In my final year at school, I developed a massive crush on my roommate in the dormitory. He was one of the school's top athletes and very handsome. Since we shared a room, I saw him naked at least twice a day and apart from being so beautiful, he was also a good friend. We sometimes went for midnight baths and he made nothing of me getting aroused when we were naked together. After long and careful consideration, I decided to tell him about my feelings. I was petrified and I hoped that he would reciprocate with feeling the same. After all, he was nice to me, so I thought he loved me too. This was not the case. However, he was very sensitive to what I told him and promised to keep my secret safe. That simple act of understanding and listening to me was one of the kindest things anyone had ever done for me. We still have sporadic contact today and I will always respect him for not judging me. For once in my life, someone unequivocally took my side.

By the time I left school, I had mastered the fine art of keeping quiet about my shame, loneliness, sadness and suicidal thoughts. As long as I kept up my performance of being happy and useful, I would be fine and perfectly acceptable. I committed to a life of 'changing myself' for the people around me because as myself, I felt that I was not good enough.

I went to university and embraced the new and exciting world that opened up to me. I had the freedom to explore my sexuality and I engaged on that level with both sexes. Even though I felt liberated, I was still in a tug of war between my deepest desires and what society, my family and the church expected of me. Deep down I had a tremendous yearning to be loved and I wanted that love to come from another man. However, just the simple thought of being intimate with a man made me feel dirty, ashamed and horrified. I hated myself and believed that the world would be a better place without me. I was unloveable, ugly and a potential disgrace to my family, and there was no hope for me to ever find happiness. I started physically harming myself.

One of my lecturers — a much older gay man — noticed the cuts and gashes on my arms, and took me under his wing. I mistook his interest in me as love. As much as I knew a romantic relationship with him would be inappropriate, my need to be loved overrode all rationality and I pursued him. He reciprocated and we entertained a short-lived secret affair. Though we never went so far as to have sex, he was the first man I got completely naked with. When it all ended I felt broken. Today, I still wonder about the roles we each played in that relationship: did he exploit my vulnerabilities or did I enable him to do so? Whatever the case may be, with his help and guidance, I stopped hurting myself and driven by a need to win back his love, I did exceptionally well in my grades.

I also looked for help and guidance in other places during this very confusing time especially in terms of finding clarity about my sexuality. I once went to a university psychologist and told her that I thought I was gay. She asked me: 'Have you had anal sex?' I said no and she responded with: 'Then you don't have a problem. I don't need to see you again.'

Once I completed my degree, I excelled in my career as a free-lance actor. I maintained a certain sense of ambiguity around my sexuality in an effort to prevent being typecast as the Pantomime Dame or the effeminate queen. I even went so far as to get involved with ex-gay ministries. I was baptised at least three times in an attempt to 'cleanse' myself from the 'terrible dark and demonic urges' I carried inside me. When these efforts didn't pay dividends, I entered a period of complete chastity.

At the same time, my search for the 'perfect wife' — one that would please my stepmom — was relentless. Since my inability to get aroused by a woman was a dead giveaway I devised all kinds of plans to avoid being exposed as a homosexual. I was so naïve as to think that if I married a woman in a wheelchair or with some other form of disability that would prevent us from having sex, I could at least live up to part of my family's expectations.

Eventually, I ran out of options and my yearning for love and companionship won the battle against religion and fundamentalism. I ended my career as an actor, moved away from my family and began to explore my life as a gay man. I discovered the club scene and Ecstasy — the dance drug. I had no mentor and entered the dark yet alluring side of gay life very quickly. By following the example set by those around me, I quickly learned how having the perfect body would give me access to the best clubs, best drugs and best-looking men. I milked the power I had as a young, sexy man and made sure that I was an object of desire.

Aged 25, I fell head over heels for an older man. In the beginning, our relationship was magical. Life felt perfect because I found someone that I loved and who loved me back. We never argued and everywhere we went people commented on what a perfect couple we were. He was the love of my life and in that cloud of euphoria, I came out to my adoptive parents by sending them a fax. For them, this was the final nail in my coffin. They certainly did not approve of my boyfriend and our lifestyle, and my relationship with my step-parents slowly deteriorated to the point that we stopped talking to one another.

After two years, my relationship with my boyfriend started to slowly derail. Our lives were consumed by too many drugs and a façade of big houses, fast cars, fabulous parties and pedigree dogs. We started to argue, jealousies and infidelities crept in and we grew apart. It dawned on me that the life we were chasing was going to destroy us and it felt that it was too late to turn on the brakes.

After three and a half years, I ended my first relationship with a feeling of disillusionment and regret. The old feelings of not wanting to be gay crept up again and I felt shameful and like a failure. Having burnt the bridges with my family, there was no one around to support me in processing the end of my relationship. I moved to a different city where I was lured deeper into the drug and club scene.

I partied harder and worked like a beast. In order to cover up how I felt inside, I did everything to maintain my outward appearance of youth and success. I lived in a great beachfront apartment and managed one of the most successful and renowned restaurants in South Africa. Cocaine became my drug of choice. It gave me confidence and enabled me to work for days on end without much sleep. My friends had free access to my house and everybody 'loved' me.

However, deep inside I was falling apart. I missed my family. I regretted the way I disregarded them when they tried to warn me against the dangers of my lifestyle and I felt there was no way to undo this damage. I blamed my homosexuality for everything that went wrong, and yet I held onto everything that was destructive about being gay. Behind closed doors, my moods became increasingly unpredictable and I suffered from severe and blinding migraines almost every week. The only way for me to control these episodes was to smoke marijuana which seemed to dull all my senses.

My drug habit was slowly destroying me and eventually I stood on the brink of losing everything. I racked up huge amounts of debt and struggled to make ends meet. I knew I needed help, but I couldn't afford rehab. I was deeply unhappy, lost and suicidal, and the drugs no longer gave me the highs I was chasing.

A friend gave me a leaflet outlining the 12 Step Programme for overcoming drug addiction. Armed with this, and as a last resort, I asked my adoptive parents if I could move in with them in preparation for relocating to London. Despite our difficult relationship, they took me in. I didn't tell them about my drug problem, because I knew it would tarnish the last bit of good in our relationship. I don't think they knew about the cold night sweats, anxiety and despair I went through in their house. But I kicked the habit. Much as my adoptive parents are unaware of the fact that they provided me with a safe haven, I am thankful that I had a place to go to — even though I had to claim it in an indirect and hidden way.

The following six months I committed to working hard, saving money and getting my affairs in order. To my surprise, my stepdad offered to help me financially. I still don't understand why he did this because he made it abundantly clear that he would never approve of me, my lifestyle and the 'choices' I had made. I know this much though: relationships are extremely complex and nothing is cut and dried when it comes to how we feel about the people in our lives — especially when we love them. Without my stepdad's help, I would not have been able to move to London and give myself a fresh start. I will always appreciate what he had done for me and realise that there must be a part of him that loves and cares about me. I am hopeful that he and I will be able to cross the bridge of our differences one day and build on a supportive and loving father-son relationship.

I spent my first four years in London in complete isolation. I worked eighteen hours a day, seven days a week, with no time to make friends or socialise. I put myself through college again, studying Graphic and Web Design, whilst working part-time as a receptionist at a publisher and pulling pints in a pub at night. I steered clear of the gay scene in an attempt to avoid drugs and other temptations. I continued smoking dope, because my migraines had now become a regular part of my life and often incapacitated me. Apart from the dopw, I was otherwise completely drug-free. I struggled to manage my moods and went from being depressed, frustrated, elated, suicidal and manic in a matter of days. My haphazard emotional state of mind made it difficult for me to allow anyone close to me and I surrendered to thinking that I was 'not a relationship person'.

Nonetheless, I excelled in my work and studies. My survival strategy, of acquiring any skill necessary to please people, served me well. Throughout my life, I have developed the un-canny knack of learning new skills and remembering things very quickly, especially when my being accepted and valued depended on it. Eventually, I achieved a lifelong dream of be-ing a writer and editor at the publishers where I started out as a receptionist.

In June 2011, I was diagnosed with mild Bipolar II Effective Disorder. In my case the culmination of childhood trauma, genetic factors, my own drug abuse and a chemical imbalance that causes tiny seizures in my brain (hence my migraines), contributed to my sometimes erratic behaviour.

I feared this diagnosis for a large part of my life, but with the help of a magnificent psychiatrist and therapist, I am beginning to put the pieces of the puzzle together. It's very much like discovering my very own 'owner's manual. It's an exciting and very rewarding journey. Sadly, I also had to learn that some people still view mental illness as a disability, a weakness or danger, and in some instances for them it as something that can be exploited. For me the biggest lesson so far has been to learn that I have the power and control to remove myself from the people and situations that make me feel emotionally unsafe. I wish I had known this earlier in my life.

My mother's death still haunts me and what happened that day still has a huge question mark hanging over it. I don't know if her death was a horrible accident or an idle threat and cry for help that went too far, or if she did in fact commit suicide. There were no witnesses who can help me remember what happened that day and it's a topic my family is hesitant to discuss. In a very real way, my mother remains part of my thoughts every day and I have to work hard not to think about the 'what ifs' and 'could have beens'.

I have a very clear memory of waking up the morning after my mother's death. I was lying next to Jonathan in his mother's bed and I had this sinking feeling of hopelessness, and I thought, 'This is not true. It did not happen.' The memory of how I felt that morning is what keeps me motivated in terms of dealing with my depression. On days when I want to give up, I remind myself that I never want someone else to wake up, feeling like the same sadness and hopelessness as a result of my actions.

Recently I found a diary inscription that my mother wrote shortly after my father died. What she wrote showed me that she loved me dearly and she had every intention to be a good parent and keep things afloat. Reading her words brought me a great sense of relief and peace, and they helped me to let go of the sadness and sense abandonment I carried for all these years. I know now that our circumstances at home were not because of anybody's wrongdoing. It was just a messed up situation.

However, I also feel ambiguous when I think about my childhood. The boy inside me wants to forgive and forget. The adult man, on the other hand, recognises the bad and abusive behaviour that happened. So it's difficult to say 'All is forgiven and forgotten', because the fact remains that as a child I was vulnerable and I needed a safe, stable, loving and nurturing environment. As much as I love them I also sit with the uncomfortable truth that my caregivers failed me in some instances.

Not too long ago I had a conversation with my stepmom. We don't speak often and when we do, we exchange platonic hallos and how-are-yous. I was reluctant to tell her about my contribution to this book for fear that she would think my aim was to publicly embarrass our family or to deliberately hurt her and my stepdad. To my surprise, when I spoke about this book she was very supportive, and she listened without being defensive or judgemental. It was a good conversation and afterwards I felt a tiny victory and a glimmer of hope for a much bigger acceptance.

I have always had complex and dysfunctional relationships with men, starting with my own father, my brother and later my stepdad. However, the most dysfunctional relationship of all of them is the one that I have had with myself, and this is the relationship that now deserves my care and attention.

For a long time I thought that I am not worthy of a loving relationship, or that I am not 'relationship person'. This influenced my choice in boyfriends and I prefered the company of men who were unreliable and emotionally distant. In recent years, I went to the other extreme and told myslef that I am incomplete without a man in my life and as a result I started choosing men that did not value and respect me. I suspect this may be because I did not value and respect myself to begin with. These bad choices perpetuated the cycle of abuse and dysfunctionality that's been a theme throughout my life, albeit by others or by myself.

With 40 approaching fast, I realise that I have not ever given myself the time and space to get to know who I truly am... know what I want from life, what my true passions are, what my dreams are, and what I look for in a romantic relationship and partner. Above all, I have not yet started to LOVE all of me, just the way I am.

A dear friend of mine always says 'When we know better, we'll do better.' Armed with those simple words I now look towards the future.

Dear Francois,

Beautiful young man, when I think of you my heart opens up and all I want to do is embrace you and tell you that you are safe.

I really wish you did not have to experience everything that happened to you as a young child. It has affected you in so many ways and as much as it pains me to say this, those events will have an influence on your life for a long time to come. But you are brave and you will pull through. Your life is a gift. Accept it, no matter how screwed up it may be sometimes.

Allow yourself to cry. Allow yourself to miss your mother and take your time to grieve. At the moment you are keeping it all inside, because you have been told that there is no point to being sad. Letting go of those emotions will make you feel less angry and it will relieve your frustration. This will help you to build a better relationship with the people who are now in your life and that want to care for you.

As much as you have good reason to be angry with your stepmom and stepdad, try to understand that they are human beings. It may seem to you that they are selfish, and in certain respects they are, but know that they work with a different set of rules. One day you will learn how difficult things are for them right now and you will regret the fact that you did not try to allow them to love you.

They will probably never understand all your complexities and that in itself frightens them as much as their ignorance infuriates you. However, their hearts are in a good place and there will come a time when you least expect it that they will step up to the mark and be there for you. So, the least you can do is to respect them.

Now let's chat about boys and love and finding that special someone. I know about your prayers, how you bargain with God and ask Him to take away your feelings. From where you are standing now, God looks like a monster.

He has already taken away so much from you and now He has given you an obstacle — your homosexuality — to overcome too. In a sense, you hate Him, because He too has forsaken you.

My dear man, this is not true. People, your caregivers and the church have a lot of catching up to do in terms of understanding who and what God is. Let me tell you now, He is inside you and is part of your spiritual DNA. You may think I am crazy for saying this, but ultimately loving yourself is the closest relationship you will ever have with God. So, stop looking for answers in places that will bring you harm. Instead, pray that one day you will find the man who is made just for you and trust that it will happen. Once you realise that you are your own creation, your life will unfold in the most wonderful ways and love WILL come.

While your current environment does not permit you to express your feelings and creativity, this will change. There will come a time when you will feel liberated and you'll start to explore everything you fantasise about now. Be careful with your own heart. Be wise about the things you are letting yourself into and learn to move away from the people who hurt you. You don't have to fall in love with the first guy who shows an interest in you, neither do you have to have sex with him straight away.

Do not dishonour yourself for the sake of being accepted by others. You will only end up betraying yourself and trust me when I tell you, the people you try to please are the ones who will love you the least. Love needs no acceptance and it lays down no tests. There's a big difference between feeling that burning lust that I know haunts you, and actually loving someone and allowing them to love you back.

This brings me to the next thing: allow people to get close to you. From where I stand now, I can tell you that the biggest lesson I've had to learn is that we work on our relationships every day and it doesn't get any easier as you grow older. The important thing is to be able to recognise which relationships are worth the effort and which ones are not; It is people's actions, not their words, that will invite you to trust them. Don't be fooled by empty promises.

The rest is up to you. Your life is your own journey. You don't have to live it for other people. When you make mistakes — oh and you will make plenty — forgive yourself first, before you look for forgiveness from others. Don't be so hard on yourself. You do not have to be perfect... and don't give others permission to tell you how you should feel about yourself.

As I write this, I look at both my arms and I see the scars of the deep wounds that you will inflict on yourself. Please do not do this. You have a beautiful body and you are amazing just the way you are. Starving, battering, bruising, and cutting yourself only make things worse.

Finally, you made a sacred contract when you entered this world. Value it and value your life. The day will come when you will make a difference to someone's life, but you need to be alive to be able to do that. The reward for helping others and allowing your light to shine is tremendous. This is my promise to you.

Be silly, laugh a lot, cry as much as you like, express your creativity with reckless abandon, use your clever mind and wicked sense of humour, and love yourself. You are extraordinary!

It is in your hands to write your story and give yourself the best life you possibly can. Dismiss those who judge you. Believe in yourself.

I love you. Don't ever forget that.

Francois

THE QUEST
Ade Adeniji

Somewhere along the way
I lost touch with myself
From being told I was flawed
From believing that I was broken
From being an outsider
Learning that being different,
meant being abnormal.

I sold out to the highest bidders
I abandoned myself
Seduced by the momentary promise
of connection and wholeness.
I locked my true self away in the abyss,
tempted down the path
of compromise and compensation.

Somewhere along the way,
I felt a deep yearning
telling me that there was more to life
than the path I was walking.
And so the Quest to finding myself began.
I came to learn that the Quest is a risk,
and that it takes courage to stay committed to the journey.

The bidders for my old self still come calling.
The seducers still play at enticing me with their nectar.
The temptations still make empty promises with their songs.
I have come to learn that the Quest is a pilgrimage,
and that it takes commitment to stay on the path.
And so here I am, on the Quest to finding my true self.

No one can make the journey for me.
It is something I must do myself.
It is not a journey I make alone,
for I have my brothers who travel with me.
Each on their own Quest
Each taking that risk to find themselves
Each unleashing the courage
to live their own authentic life.
Each committed to expressing who they are in the world.

Chapter Five

Moving Forward Authentically

Authenticity refers to one's own personal truth, sincerity, and intentions. Herein lies the problem. Everyone has his or her own unique truth and view of the world which the people around us are often ill-equipped to understand and accept.

Many of us consent to inauthentic communication, behaviour and beliefs on a daily basis. This manifests itself in the discrepancy between what we truly feel and what we communicate to others; there is a contradiction between our actions and our desires, and an inconsistency between the language we use and what we really want to express. The result is dishonouring our true selves.

Everyone else appears to be doing it and therefore it has been misunderstood as the way things are. But they are not because eventually inauthenticity becomes the source of stress, miscommunication, misunderstanding and dissatisfaction. The list goes on.

Gay men adopt an inauthentic way of living as a result of feeling oddly out of place, developing limiting beliefs and striving to survive. We learned from a very early age to hide who we truly are, to the extent that we believe this is the way things really are.

As we mentioned in the previous chapter, moving towards authenticity is indeed returning 'back home' to our true selves. However, getting to this place of 'truthful living' often means that our friends and family feel threatened by our desire to live a more integrated life. Being authentic can be incredibly challenging, because as gay men we choose to no longer play by the 'old rules' that tell us to conform, fit in and ignore our own internal voices.

Once gay men realise what the motivations behind our behaviour are (the ones that no longer serve us or satisfy our needs), we feel an urge to become truthful and whole. Authenticity cuts through historical, cultural, religious and societal rules. It is indeed a breaking of chains and an escape from the prison of our old beliefs and survival mechanisms. In this sense, authenticity is a revolutionary force that demands a level of personal awareness coupled with an equally powerful freedom of expression.

In some ways, living authentically is similar to how young children who are not yet inhibited by the world around them, say things as they see and feel them. However, as adults, when we return to our true selves, we are able to blend a generous amount of experience, knowledge and communication skills with this child-like freedom of expression. This enables us to retain and nurture a healthy connection with our personal needs; life becomes a dance between our awareness and our experience.

With our limiting beliefs and survival strategies still firmly in place, gay men are unable to move gracefully across their own personal 'authentic ballroom'. We are so busy reacting against the things we don't want that we stop creating the life we really want and strive to live. For many, it is only in our later years, after we have accumulated success, achievement and experience that we look back, reflect on our lives and ask ourselves this critical question: 'Is this really what I wanted and does it truly make me feel fulfilled?'

Once we've asked this question, it may dawn on us that in fact we wanted something completely different. This is particularly true for many gay men as they realise that they've strived, battled, persisted, struggled, repeated old patterns of behaviours and continually applied themselves throughout their lives with a bundle of beliefs, fears and strategies which have not served them in the way they really wanted. It is hardly surprising that gay men are often ill-prepared to embrace the joys and challenges of being an adult or to experience the power of authentic living.

To experience the power and joy of finding our way back home and dancing to our own music, we have to first investigate the past, explore the present and release any deep-seated pain so that we can create a new and authentic life. In this final stage of our journey, we challenge and dissolve old beliefs and establish new nurturing habits as we shed old relationships and create new ones.

The answers, solutions and behaviours we discover as we deconstruct our lives can be surprising. We may experience radical changes in our lifestyle, find ourselves in new and unchartered territory and start to feel differently about ourselves and the world we inhabit. We enter the realm of transformation. This is often a confusing place to be in. Everything we thought we knew is open for questioning. We might even be frightened of this new experience and as we look at ourselves differently and the world starts to transform around us, we may ask ourselves: 'how do I do this?'

The pursuit of living an authentic life is something all human beings can engage in when they ask themselves the key critical questions: 'who am I ?' and 'what do I want?'. We get closer to the answers to those questions by listening to the creative response we feel when we ask them. By applying practice, patience, perseverance and the belief that our inner voice will honour and elevate our true self, we invite authenticity into our lives.

Shakespeare states it beautifully when he delivers the words 'to thine own self be true.'

CHAPTER SIX

RESOURCES:
FINDING SUPPORT

In some instances, growing up gay today is not such a big deal. The world is changing and never before in history has homosexuality enjoyed as much media coverage as it does today. In many places, all over the world, social attitudes are changing and as a result our community enjoys liberation. That's a good thing! However, life is not a great big glitter ball for everyone. For many of us, life is still a struggle and support can be difficult to find. In this section we list organisations across the world that work towards making life easier for gay people.

While we made every effort to list organisations from as many regions in the world as possible, we know that some will not be mentioned here. Luckily, there are international organisations that will make an effort to help you or point you in the right direction should you not find one listed in your own country.

As an alternative, we will also keep this section updated on our website and we invite anybody to add organisations we may have missed on this list, by simply leaving a comment on this page:

www.lovemeasiamthebook/finding-support/

INTERNATIONAL ORGANISATIONS

The following international organisations work toward the equality of lesbian, gay, bisexual, trans and intersex (LGBTI) people and their liberation from all forms of discrimination.

ILGA — International Lesbian, Gay, Bisexual, Trans and Intersex Association — Focuses public and government attention on cases of discrimination against LGBTI people by supporting programmes and protest actions, asserting diplomatic pressure, providing information and working with international organisations and the international media.

Website: http://ilga.org
Contact: information@ilga.org

Stonewall — A lesbian, gay and bisexual rights charity in the United Kingdom named after the Stonewall Inn of Stonewall riots fame. It is the largest gay equality organisation not only in the UK but also in Europe.

Website: www.stonewall.org.uk
Contact: info@stonewall.org.uk

IGLHRC— International Gay and Lesbian Human Rights Commission — A US-based international non-governmental organisation that addresses human rights violations against lesbians, gay men, bisexuals, intersexuals, transgender people and people with HIV/AIDS. It is accredited by the United Nations and holds consultative status with that organisation.

Website: www.iglhrc.org
Contact: iglhrc@iglhrc.org (US), mena@iglhrc.org (Africa/ Middle East), asia@iglhrc.org (Asia), lac@iglhrc.org (South America)

ORGANISATIONS FOR ARAB COUNTRIES

Gay and Lesbian Arabic Society (GLAS)

An international organisation established in 1988 in the US that serves as a networking organisation for Gays and Lesbians of Arab descent or those living in Arab countries. They aim to promote positive images of Gays and Lesbians in Arab communities worldwide, in addition to combating negative portrayals of Arabs within the Gay and Lesbian community. They also provide a support network for members. They are part of the global Gay and Lesbian movement seeking an end to injustice and discrimination based on sexual orientation.

Website: www.glas.org

ORGANISATIONS LISTED BY COUNTRY

Australia

National LGBTI Health Alliance Members — A coalition of organisations from across Australia which provide health-related programmes, services and research targeting lesbian, gay, bisexual, transgender, intersex and other sexuality, sex and gender diverse people.

Phone: (02) 8568 1120
Website: www.lgbthealth.org.au
Contact: info@lgbtihealth.org.au

Brazil

Grupo Gay da Bahia — The Gay Group of Bahia is the oldest of its kind in Brazil and was founded in 1980. It's a non-profit organisation and is a member of the International Lesbian and Gay Association and forms part of the International Lesbian and Gay Human Rights Commission.

Website: www.ggb.org.br
Contact: ggb@ggb.org.br

Canada

Egale Canada (formerly Equality for Gays And Lesbians Everywhere) — An advocacy organisation founded in 1986 to advance equality for Canadian LGBT people and their families, across Canada. Egale's work includes lobbying for more equitable laws for LGBT people, intervening in legal cases that have an impact on human rights and equality, and increasing public education and awareness by providing information to individuals, groups, and media. Egale has over 3,300 members including people in every province and territory of Canada.

Website: http://archive.egale.ca/
Contact egale.canada@egale.ca

France

Inter-LGBT (Interassociative Lesbienne, Gaie, Bi et Trans) is an umbrella group of 50 LGBT organisations in France.

Website: www.inter-lgbt.org

India

Udaan Trust — A non-governmental organisation operating in the state of Maharashtra and the first HIV/AIDS organisation founded by homosexuals living with HIV/AIDS. Udaan focuses on issues of sexual health within the homosexual and transgendered communities, particularly with regard to the prevention of HIV/AIDS. In order to accomplish this, Udaan provides services such as condom distribution, sex education, counselling, and medical services to at-risk populations.

Website: www.udaantrust.org

Ireland

LGBT Diversity — The LGBT Diversity programme is a co-ordinated response by twelve LGBT organisations in Ireland, developed to build the capacity of the LGBT sector. The programme will facilitate LGBT organisations and activists to collectively mobilise and engage with the wider community in order to advocate strategically and effectively on gender and sexuality issues.

Website: www.lgbtdiversity.com

LGBT Helpline — Provides access to trained volunteers who provide a non-judgemental, confidential, listening support and information service for lesbian, gay, bisexual and transgender (LGBT) people as well as their family and friends. Their website also provides a gateway to information and support options for LGBT people in Ireland.

Phone: 042-9329816
Website: www.lgbt.ie
Contact: info@lgbt.ie

Russia

Russian LGBT network — Interregional non-governmental organisation working for the protection of rights and social adaptation of sexual and LGBT gender minorities. The network structure includes 13 regional branches and 10 regional LGBT organisations.

Website: www.lgbtnet.ru

South Africa

The Lesbian and Gay Equality Project (LGEP) — A non-profit organisation that works for full legal and social equality for LGBTI people in South Africa. The LGEP was formerly known as the National Coalition for Gay and Lesbian Equality.

Website: www.equality.org.za
Contact: info@equality.org.za

Uganda

Civil Society Coalition on Human Rights and Constitutional Law

Established in October 2009 in response to the tabling of a now notorious Anti-Homosexuality Bill in the Ugandan Parliament, was one of the winners of the 2011 Human Rights Defenders Award, awarded by the US Department of State.

Website: www.ugandans4rights.org
Contact: info@ugandans4rights.org

United Kingdom

Albert Kennedy Trust — Supports LGBT young people in crisis and works to ensure that they are able to live in accepting, supportive and caring homes, by providing a range of services to meet the individual needs of those who would otherwise be homeless or living in a hostile environment.

Website: www.akt.org.uk

Elton John Aids Foundation (EJAF) — Established in the United States in 1992 and along with EJAF in the UK, pursues the same mission – to reduce the incidence of HIV/AIDS through innovative HIV prevention programmes, efforts to eliminate stigma and discrimination associated with HIV/AIDS, and direct treatment and care services for people living with HIV/AIDS.

Website: www.ejaf.org

Galop — London's leading anti-LGBT hate crime charity, making life safe, just and fair for LGBT people.

Website: www.galop.org.uk
Contact: info@galop.org.uk

Pace Health — The charity promotes the mental health and emotional well-being of the LGBT community and is committed to researching the changing needs of LGBT people, and offering wide ranging, crucial support services to meet these needs and help people move through their difficult times.

Website: www.pacehealth.org.uk

LLGS Switchboard — London Lesbian & Gay Switchboard provides a range of services for the LGBT community. Their aim is to provide an information, support and referral service for LGBT people and anyone who needs to consider issues around their sexuality.

Helpline: 0300 330 0630 (Daily 10am - 11pm)
Website: www.llgs.org.uk
This link on ther website, www.turingnetwork.org.uk, provides a directory of LGBT health services across the UK.

Terrence Higgins Trust — The charity's vision is a world where people with HIV live healthy lives free from prejudice and discrimination, and good sexual health is a right and reality for all. The Terrence Higgins Trust is generally considered the UK's leading HIV and AIDS charity, and the largest in Europe.

Call Direct: 0808 802 1221
Website: www.tht.org.uk
Contact: info@tht.otg.uk

United States

Out & Equal — Works to achieve workplace equality for all regardless of sexual orientation, gender identity, expression, or characteristics. In addition, Out & Equal provides training and sensitivity resources to LGBT employees and corporations alike through advocacy, training programmes and events.

Call Direct: (415) 694.6500
Website: www.outandequal.org
Contact: info@outandequal.org

National Gay and Lesbian Task Force — Founded in 1973, this non-profit organisation works to build the grassroots power of the LGBT community.

Website: www.thetaskforce.org
Contact: info@TheTaskForce.org

National Coalition of Anti-Violence Programmes (NCAVP) — A national organisation dedicated to reducing violence and its impacts on LGBT individuals in the US.

Website: www.avp.org

The Trevor Project — The Trevor Project is the leading national organisation, in the US, providing crisis intervention and suicide prevention services to LGBT teenagers, and anyone who needs to consider issues around their sexuality.

Crisis Helpline: 1-866-488-7386
Trevor Lifeline: 866-4.U.TREVOR [866.488.7386]

Telephone Contact:
Los Angeles: 310.271.8845
Main (Fax): 310.271.8846
New York: 212.509.0072

Website: www.thetrevorproject.org

I

nformation was accurate at the time of publishing.

ABOUT
THE QUEST

The Quest is an exceptional resource for gay men to explore and better understand the complexities, joys, challenges, frustrations, thinking and emotions involved with being a gay man in today's world.

Spearheaded by founders, Ade Adeniji and Darren Brady, two experienced Life Coaches and Group Facilitators, The Quest is helping gay men to rediscover their authentic selves and re-defining the meaning of community within gay London. From within a supportive and safe environment, alongside a diverse range of individuals, The Quest's work enriches relationships, with a deeper understanding of personal interactions and mo-tivations, through self-acceptance, new possibilities and social awareness.

The Quest offers a diverse range of services that include a variety of workshops, 1-1 coaching and more relaxed social events, which cater for all kinds of curiosity.

The Weekend Exploration for Gay Men is the flagship work-shop offered by The Quest. The Exploration involves taking participants on a journey through their lives, using a map with four 'ports of call'. This process involves 'investigating' the past by looking at the significant moments and experiences that occurred in childhood, adolescence and early adulthood.

'Exploring' the present, this time looking at how the participants show up in their respective lives. Then, there are opportunities to 'release' any toxicity that is not helping to create a life of fulfillment and vitality. And finally, participants 'cultivate' the insights and tools to help them live their own definition of an authentic life.

In addition, The Quest provides ongoing support to participants post-attendance, including a range of complementary services, such as the 'WorkOUT' sessions. Each WorkOUT focuses on a specific theme and is an opportunity for participants to reconnect to the power of the Weekend Exploration and continue sustaining the momentum for authentic living.

For more information about The Quest, visit:
www.thequestawaitsyou.com

Note From The Editor

When I started this project, I had no idea where this journey would take me. I had already met most of the contributors through The Quest and was familiar with what they had written. So the task ahead of me seemed easy: Collect their letters and turn them into a book.

However, I soon learned that these men had so much more to say apart from writing a few words of love, encouragement and understanding to their younger selves. As I interviewed the individual contributors, it became clear to me that in the shadow of each letter lay a life storie aching to be told. I realised that it would be a great disservice to these men if they did not get the opportunity to find their own voices and speak their personal truth.

The subject matter is not an easy one and the lives laid bare in this book are not those of celebrities or media personalities — glamourising their truth was not an option for the contributors. Instead, all they were armed with was the raw honesty of their childhood experiences and how it impacted their adult lives. As a result none of them set out to tell romantic and beautiful stories.

At times it was a difficult process because many of the memories they had to delve into are easier to lock away than to face head on, let alone share with an unknown public audience. However, it was interesting to observe that as they documented their lives, the contributors all had a sense of liberation. This new sense of freedom — of being unburdened — became the driving force for them to persist in their goal: To share their stories and colourful history and to testify to the world that it's OK to be different, in the hope that young gay teenagers who are still bogged down by homophobia and prejiduce can have a better future.

Since creating *Love Me As I Am* was such a deeply personal experience for the contributors and myself, we also wanted the book to be an intimate conversation between the reader and each of these men. I tried to retain each contributor's unique voice as far as possible and I allowed them to write as they would speak.

It would've been much easier to give the reader a quick impression of the contributors by showing photographs along with their biographies and letters. After all, a picture paints a thousand words. However, photographs leave very little to the imagination and can often taint our judgement. Words, on the other hand, are some of the most powerful and lasting memories we keep of a person. Once someone's face, voice and touch have faded from our memories, it is his or her words that still linger in our minds.

Each contributor added a quote at the beginning of his story — something that resonates with him, be it the words of a famous author, a television character or something he says to himself as a mantra. We credited the quotes to the people who have said them and where it was not possible to trace back their origin, we noted them as anonymous. In many cases, the actual source of the quotes was ambiguous, so we left out all sources for reasons of continuity.

To my knowledge this is the first time that an anthology of writings like *Love Me As I Am* has been documented in the UK. It is my wish that the stories of these ordinary men will allow you to see into their hearts and souls, and that the tapestry of their beautiful lives will make a lasting imprint on your own.

Sincerely yours,

Francois Lubbe
Editor

CONTRIBUTING AUTHORS

CHAPTER ONE:
ODDLY OUT OF PLACE

Phil Garrood — 47: going on 12. A lover of sport, dogs and a nice cup of tea. He's not sure what he wants to be when he grows up. London born and bred and still lives there in sunny Marylebone.

Gavin McGregor — 35: and still not sure who he is. On the outside, he's a former journalist, political researcher, and now a charity fundraiser for an environmental education charity. On the inside, he feels most at peace when foraging for wild food, fingers sticky with brambles and stung by nettles. He lives in London with his partner of seven years.

Fernando De Assis — 42: An ex-restaurateur who left his good job in the city of London back in 2010 to dedicate himself to his great passion, which is managing a charity that looks after the welfare of cats and dogs in the streets of Recife/Brazil. He lives in London where he is studying 'The Knowledge' to become a taxi driver. He enjoys yoga, vipassana meditation and lives alone with his two cats, Nina and Amy. He is very reserved and content with life, though he is still learning and always will.

Andrew Courten — 54: Successful business man in the IT industry. He is now financially independent based on the profits he made and runs several homes in town and country; loving world opera, culture, Bentleys, philosophy, skiing and scuba, fun clubs. He runs many diverse projects and spends 20 per cent of the year travelling the world. He lived with his first partner for 27 years until his sudden, shattering death. After the passing of his first partner, Andrew challenged the homophobic inheritance laws in the Strasbourg Human Rights Court and the UK, and won. He has now been married to his lawyer for five years. Love and life are beautiful and related.

José Veiga — 39: A Health Coach and Mental Health Worker who is British born of Portuguese descent. He lives in London and loves meditation, travelling and harbours dreams of travelling the world and being swept off his feet by that special man.

Christopher Nichols — 40: He is in unchartered waters as he stands at a pivotal point in his life. He finds it extraordinary that for a significant amount of time, he valued so many external things and social status all in an effort to prove himself. Once he realised how this grandiosity enslaved him into addiction, he reluctantly had to let it all go to save himself from a slow demise. Now, at the age of 40, after losing everything, he has returned to the same place he was at age 16. Back then, he left home armed with only his illusions of the world based on his life experiences, and set out to establish a life for himself. Today, the same is true about his life. Having been to hell and back, he is thankful to still be alive today. Like Michael Jackson, Chris feels he now is starting with the man in the mirror... asking him to change his ways... If you want to make the world a better place, take a look at yourself, and then make a change, holds true for him.

Chapter Two:
Developing Limiting Beliefs

Ade Adeniji - 44: Coach, Group Facilitator, Co-founder of The Quest. Also storyteller and improviser. Born in London, and spent his late childhood and adolescence in Nigeria. An explorer at heart, he spent many years searching for himself, only to recently discover that he was never lost, he had simply been hiding from himself. He divides his time between London and Amsterdam, where he lives with his partner.

Ian Patrick — 55: The lost and found department. Runs a charity for his sins "Miracle Network" (www.miracles.org.uk), which he founded, so only has himself to blame. Trained as a geologist, worked in the oil industry; loves to travel and get involved in theatre, especially as an actor; and has just had his first book published — "*Of Course! How Many Light Bulbs Does It Take to Change?: Reflections on A Course in Miracles*". His only ambition is to be happy.

Paul Woodward — 45: Senior university lecturer in Theatre, Director, Writer and Workshop Leader. He lived in London most of his adult life but recently packed his bags to follow his heart and dreams, and flew to Melbourne, Australia. Currently Paul is studying for his PhD entitled 'The Performativity of (dis)closure' in which he is attempting to marry performance theory with storytelling to create a poetics of disclosure which will help people breach their inner/outer world personas and histories with confidence, clarity, courage and compassion.

Robert Ramcharan — 48: Works as a contractor within the banking industry specialising in Market Risk. A Roman Catholic of South Asian descent and originally hailing from Trinidad, West Indies. Rob has two kids aged 15 and 18, having been in a committed marriage for over 20 years. He separated from his English wife and is now living an openly gay life, in London. He maintains a great relationship with his ex-wife and they are both an important part of each other's lives. Rob loves keeping fit and travelling. His hope is that his story has an impact on other gay married men struggling to cope with their preference and the implications of abiding by the norms of a heterosexual society. Rob loves a challenge and now loves daring to be different.

Tim Poole— 51: A psychotherapist with his own practice. Despite having a rough start in his younger years, he finally feels that he has found his direction. It's taken him a while but he's now doing something which means a lot to him. He didn't get much help when he was younger but struggled through; life is tough sometimes but it doesn't always have to be. Being able to talk about his feelings has helped him enormously and if he can do that for someone else, so much the better. www.timpoolecounselling.co.uk

Neil Thomas — 55: Decent, honest, law-abiding, loving, happy and admirable. This is what we all aspire to be. We fail. Why? The aspiration for beauty doesn't make us beautiful... Neil is funny, enjoys being naughty, and loves partying with his many great, lovely, close friends. Blissfully partnered with a man who came into his life just at the right time to be able to be fully appreciated. As he approaches retirement, he hopes to move away from the service industry — serving and pleasing others, and to possibly find a new direction with something more meaningful and more personal to individuals: Massage, Reiki, Cognitive behaviour therapy, Emotional Freedom Technique, Life coaching, and Electro-magnetic field balancing technique. In mastering these healing techniques and empowerment skills, he hopes to help people who are ready to move on from the pain, destructive habits and addictions in their lives.

CHAPTER THREE:
STRIVING TO SURVIVE

David Watson — 48: Ex-IT professional, ex-property search agent, ex-small time club promoter who spent the last few years struggling with health issues, but is now well and wondering what to do next. Originally from Northern England (Nelson, Lancashire) he spent periods living in the USA and Berlin, but is now firmly settled in London. You're most likely to meet him walking his dog, Guinness, in Kennington Park.

Giampiero Sanna — 36: He is a Travel Agent, originally from Italy, who is now living in London where he works for a travel agency. Apart from discovering new places, he has a great passion for theatre and in his free time takes singing and drama courses with the ambition of fulfilling his dream of acting on stage one day. In London, he enjoys the privilege of living in a lively city, which has given him the chance of meeting great people with whom he established some very important relationships. Giampiero believes that it is possible to make the most of life by living each day as an amazing discovery. He will never stop the learning process and he hopes to always get the best from life and share it with his family and friends.

John Holt — 58: A proud Lancastrian who followed a pretty random design career to live and work in New York, Singapore and Moscow but is now happily home and trying to make the most of living in London. He occasionally rafts on the Zambezi, sings at Sydney Opera House, or goes dog-sledding in the Arctic. His few remaining ambitions are turning in to a bucket list and he's alarmed to find that in '100 places to see before you die' he's well over half-way through.

Darren Brady — 47: Coach, Co-founder of The Quest, native Mancunian and latter-day Londoner. He was the kid in the street who organised the games, activities and puppet shows. He now does the same in adult form in dynamic group workshops and powerful coaching sessions that demand the same energy and involvement.

Neil Rothwell — 45: Born in Lancashire. Lives and works in London as a freelance Hairstylist and Make-up Artist. Currently studying the art of performance, trampolining and science of the mind. He lives for the day, loves beautiful places filled with life... and dreams of returning home to a 1977 International 31ft Airstream Trailer, parked by a lake.

Ronny P. — 38: Originally from Berlin but lives in London. He is a self-identified neo-realist with an academic background in International Relations with French and Modern History; practising language teacher, and aspiring social commentator/writer. He's done most of the things on his mental to-do list, sometimes misses his HIV-negative self, and lives every year as if it were his last...

CHAPTER FOUR:
STRIVING TO SURVIVE

Anton Philips — 42: A practical and sensitive guy, very creative and interested in fine art, science, engineering, and creating things in general. He keeps fit and enjoys sports like windsurfing and cycling, and has a desire to fly one day. Anton has been in a long term relationship for over 12 years. His partner has two children. His mantra for life is: to be free, to be me, and express all I am, and can be.

Blake Askew — 36: A professional actor/singer who grew up in South Africa where he ended up getting involved in ex-gay ministries from an evangelical church environment. It took him a while to see the light but he now resides in London as a professional performer and also is openly gay. He loves cats, loathes the musical *CATS* and while still a Christian, has a more liberal approach to things. He hasn't grown up really, seeing that being an actor demands a childlike state.

David Manning – 48: Moved to London from West Wales at 19, and is still engaged in an on-going love affair with the city. He really appreciates connecting with nature, and runs a small garden design company. He is enjoying storytelling, and reframing perspectives on his past, and opening to brighter possibilities for the future. He wants to own a place by the sea, preferably the Mediterranean.

Daniel Muñoz — 47: Graphic designer and web developer, originally from Spain. He lives in London where he works in a Design Studio. He misses mum and Spanish food but loves

London's rainy weather. He would love to visit outer space one day and after a series of difficult relationships, he still believes in love.

Tyrone — 45: He's happiest when travelling to new places, climbing and exploring the outdoors, or cooking. He strongly dislikes dishonest, pushy and self-centred people and believes no-one should have to put up with those who display these characteristics... just walk away and stay true to yourself.

Francois Lubbe - 37: Writer, artist, poet and painter who is originally from South Africa. He got lost for a while and now lives happily in London where he works as a writer and editor. Francois is happiest when he makes things with his hands and he still wants to design and build his own house, adopt a child, make a movie and learn how to fly a hot air balloon.

ACKNOWLEDGEMENTS

The following UK-based organisations have been invaluable in their continuing support of The Quest: GMFA - the gay men's health charity, Living Well, Positive Health Scheme (Central YMCA), Foyles Bookstore, Gay's The Word, TimeOut London, Pink Therapy UK and Kairos London.

All the previous participants of The Quest workshops, and the ever-expanding group of people who have made a special effort to support The Quest including: Gaetan, Paul W, Eyndia, Chris, Neil, Richard, Mark, Barrie, Ilyas, Chris S, Sian Jones, Paul B, Troy, Alice, James, Joseph, Alex, Positive Heath team, Bloomsbury Patients Network, Jake, and Homolab.

Amito Haarhuis, Michael Laniyan, Bettina Duske, Jo Lawrence and David Omari for putting their belief in Ade, and their consistent support.

Susan for being Darren's weekly set of ears, Moira for reminding him of who he is, Joyce for giving him spirit and determination, the School for Social Entrepreneurs for inspiring him, Jamie for their unique chats and Andrew for providing him with a place to retreat to.

Heidi Hutchence and Monalee Otto-Stadelman for always being a constant in Francois' life, Sinead Hurley for her personal support and expert advice, Nicolette Pool for simply saying 'Yes you can!' and waiting for him at the finishing line and Jacqui Scott-Burgen for being a dear friend and surrogate mother.

Special thanks go to Linda Hardingham for her design input — especially in terms of the cover design, Ian Patrick for his editorial support, Carolyne Roberts for the care and time she took to proofread the manuscript and John Holt for kindly covering the cost of her services.

REFERENCES

CHAPTER ONE: ODDLY OUT OF PLACE

1. *Belonging: Including Children of Gay and Lesbian Parents — and All Children — in Your Program*, by Aimee Gelnaw, published online in 2005, aimeegelnaw.com/Belonging.pdf

2. *Newsweek's Andrew Sullivan on Barack Obama: The First Gay President*, published 13.05.2012

3. *When Your 7-Year-Old Son Announces, 'I'm Gay'*, by Amelia, published online 02.16.12, huffingtonpost.com

CHAPTER TWO: DEVELOPING LIMITING BELIEFS

1. *Stonewall's School Report 2012*, published online, stonewall.org.uk/schoolreport2012.

2. *Battling the Bullies*, published online by Good Men Project Magazine, goodmenproject.com, 05.10.10

3. *Why do we judge based on sexuality?*, by Miller, B. published online, October 11, 2004, toledoblade.com

4. *Portrayal of Homosexuality in the Media*, by A. Shapiro, M. Schultz, C. Roush, C. Shofar, E. Shilling, T. Simpson & N. Sampiller, published Bowling Green State University, 2004, bgsu.edu/departments/tcom/faculty/ha/tcom103fall2004/gp16/gp16.pdf

Chapter Three: Striving to Survive

1. *Gay and Bisexual Men's Health Survey, April 2012*

2. *American Psychological Association - What is sexual orientation? Published online:*
apa.org